The LNER 2-6-0 Classes

The LNER
2-6-0 Classes

John F. Clay & J. Cliffe

LONDON

IAN ALLAN LTD

First published 1978

ISBN 0 7110 0844 2

Published by Ian Allan Ltd, Shepperton, Surrey,
and printed in the United Kingdom by
Crampton & Sons Ltd, Sawston Cambridge.

Contents

	Preface	6
1	The History of the 2-6-0 Type	7
2	The Ancestry of the First Great Northern 2-6-0 Mixed Traffic Engine	12
3	The Two-Cylinder Gresley Moguls	16
4	The K3 Class Moguls	22
5	Moguls on the West Highland	34
6	Mogul Performance	44
7	Moguls in Perspective	58
	Appendices	64
	Bibliography	80

Preface

The bulk of the work of this world is performed not by the great and the brilliant, but by hoards of ordinary people. In the same way most of the work on the railway was performed by ordinary locomotives. No class of locomotive has been a more typical work horse than the 2-6-0 type. On the LNER the type was used on all classes of traffic, from the humble loose coupled freight to all but the fastest of passenger trains. For many years Mogul class engines hauled the fastest fitted freight trains in the country on LNER lines. In course of time the development of the larger V2 class 2-6-2 locomotives caused the 2-6-0s to take a rather lower place in the LNER order of precedence, but the last LNER Mogul design, the K1 of 1949, proved to be among the best freight engines for its size.

For information our thanks are due to Messrs P. H. V. Banyard, M. Boddy, Lt-Col K. Cantlie, G. W. Carpenter, S. Checkley, R. N. Clements, J. D. Cliffe, P. J. Coster, H. A. Gamble, R. H. N. Hardy, G. H. K. Lund, K. R. Phillips, J. W. P. Rowledge, W. O. Skeat, J. Storr, P. N. Townend, S. C. Townroe, E. D. Trask and any others who, through inefficiency rather than for malice, we may have omitted. Without their help no book could have been produced.

We also thank the Editor of *The Railway Magazine* for permission to quote from articles in past issues, especially those of the late C. S. Lake. We have received valuable help from the staff at the British Transport Historical Records section and especially from the Librarian of the Institution of Mechanical Engineers, S. G. Morrison and his staff,

We are most grateful to the various photographers who have brought life to the book, especially T. G. Hepburn who has once more given freely from his vast collection and to K. Montague of the Special Projects Section of the BR Public Relations Dept for permission to publish the line drawing of the small K6 type Mogul which was designed but never built.

Leicester   *J. F. Clay*
London   *J. Cliffe*
April 1978

CHAPTER ONE

The History of the 2-6-0 Type

The 2-6-0 was, in all essentials, the true working class engine. It made its first appearance in 1842 and was at first used for slow freight haulage, but developed later into a mixed traffic type built continuously in the United States from soon after 1860 to 1910. In later times it was considered too small for such work in America, but many 2-6-0s were employed on goods and mixed traffic duties in other parts of the world. The first British 2-6-0s were built for freight haulage with only occasional use on relatively slow passenger trains. Britain also built numbers of such engines for export. From 1910 onwards, just as the type was being outclassed in the US, a number of British railways built 2-6-0s intended for faster running than was expected of the type anywhere else in the world. Speeds of up to 80mph have been recorded by a number of 2-6-0 classes in this country and such engines have deputised on express trains at times of heavy traffic on some quite fast express services. The LNER examples have been among the fastest of all.

It would appear that the very first 2-6-0 was built in 1842 in the United States by Eastwick and Harrison for use on heavy freight services in Russia. From the engraving it seems to have an early form of radial truck, although the sideways movement was limited by the position of the outside cylinders. In this respect it was in advance of some slightly later examples. Among the first 2-6-0s built for use in the US were six engines built by James Millholland for the Philadelphia and Reading RR. The first appeared in 1852 and later examples were added in 1855. Their leading carrying wheels were very close to the leading driving wheels and were behind the cylinders in one rigid frame. They were only suitable for slow, heavy mineral traffic. They were among the first locomotives adapted for anthracite coal and the Millholland patent firebox was mounted behind the driving wheels. Later a few 2-6-0s were built with a two-wheeled truck ahead of the cylinders but still in a rigid frame.

The 2-6-0 type, as we know it, was really developed after the introduction of the centre pin bolster permitting lateral movement of the leading axle soon after 1860. The resulting engine had more adhesion weight than the typical contemporary American 4-4-0 and was a cheaper engine to build than a 4-6-0. An engine typical of the early mixed traffic 2-6-0 was built by the Baldwin Locomotive Works in 1870, driving wheels were 4ft 6in in diameter and equalising beams were employed as a concession to lightly laid track. The more rigid

7

contemporary British track made the 0-6-0 a more popular locomotive at this period.

The 2-6-0 appeared fairly early in France and the Paris-Orleans Railway built some long-lived examples in 1885 with outside Gooch valve gear. A notable example was a three-cylinder compound 2-6-0 built by the Nord in 1887. It was number 3.101 and it predated the later Smith three-cylinder compounds built in Britain by having an inside high pressure cylinder, the opposite of Webb's contemporary engines.

Although 2-6-0s had been built for export overseas, the first examples built for a British company appeared on the Great Eastern Railway. They were originally designed by W. Adams before his departure for the L&SWR, but various modifications were added by Massey Bromley. There is little doubt that American practice had been studied and the general appearance was very different from contemporary British goods engines. The first example appeared from Neilson's in 1878. The leading pony truck was similar to that used on the Pennsylvania RR. Driving wheel tyres were omitted on the centre pair but these were replaced later by flanged tyres. The engines were numbered 527-541, and Nos 527-531 had additional sand boxes on the boiler giving them an even more un-British appearance. These were however removed after a few month's service. The valves placed above the cylinders were of the Webb circular pattern intended to prevent grooves or unequal wear. Similar valves were used on a number of LNWR engines and on the Massey Bromley 4-2-2s. A type of circular valve was patented by Church and used on some Fowler and Marshall traction engines, but whether used on road or rail the fate was the same, excessive wear and occasional seizure limited any hopes for future development.

The GER 2-6-0 was a bold design which was, in many ways, ahead of its time. The rocker arrangement used to drive the outside valves was almost identical to that used with success by Churchward much later, while the steam brakes and side windowed cab were advances on contemporary standards. Unfortunately they did not fulfil expectations. They were intended for the Peterborough to London coal traffic routed via March but they were not a success. They were, reputedly, sluggish on the road, poor steamers and heavy on coal. Unplanned stops had sometimes to be made at Cambridge to take on coal and at times they had to berth their trains in sidings and run light to Stratford to refuel and find the energy to return and complete their journeys. The older Johnson 0-6-0s, although less powerful and unable to haul the maximum loads given to a 2-6-0, showed greater overall economy. It is unfortunate that a design of considerable potential capacity should have been such a disappointment, but the fact that they were all scrapped between 1885-7 shows the extent of GER disapproval. It appears that cylinder condensation was a problem, possibly owing to the exposed outside valve chest. There was some criticism of bad workmanship with leaking boilers. They may well have been built down to a price as the 'Swedie' had its financial troubles at this time. For many years afterwards the GER limited their freight engine building to comparatively small 0-6-0s. The tenders from the 2-6-0s were used on Class Y14 0-6-0s and some lasted until 1916.

The first engine of the class, No 527, had the name 'Mogul' on the large sandboxes over the middle pair of driving wheels. At this period the Great Mogul of Delhi was very much in the public eye, but it may not be true to claim that the association of the name 'Mogul' with the 2-6-0 type had its origin in engine No 527. There are engravings of American 2-6-0s of much earlier date with the words 'Mogul Type Engine'. In the eyes of the general public any American engine built for high power rather than for high speed gained the name 'Mogul' just as, at a later date, all high speed locomotives became for a short time 'Atlantics', The word 'Mogul' has often been misused in Western fiction. In America the 2-6-0 was relatively a very small engine.

Following the scrapping of the GER Moguls this country was without any 2-6-0s until 1895 when two small Moguls intended for export to a defaulting company in South America were sold by Beyer Peacock to the Midland and South Western Junction Railway. Towards the end of the century there was something of a locomotive famine in Britain and neither company workshops nor outside builders could accept any more work. The Great Northern, the Great Central and the Midland ordered some 2-6-0 goods engines from America. Those from the GNR and the GCR were built by Burnham and Williams at the Baldwin Locomotive Works in Philadelphia. They were slightly smaller than the earlier GER Moguls and their 18in × 24in cylinders were much smaller than the 19in × 26in of the Adams/Massey Bromley engines. GNR records show that their purchases cost £2,418 each.

The GNR and the GCR each had 20 American-built Moguls in 1899-1900. The GNR batch, numbered 1181-1200, were assembled at Ardsley shed and spent most of their time working coal trains in the Leeds district but later some were used in the Nottingham area and a few were stationed at Hornsea shed towards the end of their lives. A photograph has been published showing one of them working a close-coupled suburban train. Scrapping of the GNR examples commenced in 1911 with Nos 1185/6/90.

The GCR engines were assembled at Gorton, where most of them were stationed; others were at Lincoln and New Holland while, later, a few were at Leicester working mainly on goods trains to Brunswick and Ardsley. They were sometimes used on ballast trains. At holiday periods they would take 14 or more six-wheeled coaches to Cleethorpes via Killamarsh. They also took turns on local services to Nottingham, Rugby and Woodford. The GCR had a power classification system which had the highest power associated with the lowest numbers. The 'Yankee' Moguls were Class 4 while the saturated 0-6-0 'Pom-Poms' were Class 3.

Drivers appreciated the cab comfort, especially in bad weather, and although the boiler projected backwards into the cab, making it less roomy than it looked, it was still much better than contemporary British standards. Firing had to be carried out with care as the firebox was on the narrow side. The firing shovel had to be turned almost sideways to avoid all the coal falling into the firebox centre. The double bogied tenders were of less dead weight than an English six-wheeled tender of equal capacity owing to the use of thinner plates in the building of the water tanks. American features of design, such as bar frames and equalising bars, were not popular, but before the steam locomotives had ended it career in Britain there were proposals to introduce both into some of the standard locomotives of the early 1950s. Professional locomotive engineers are not at all convinced that the faithful adherence to British plate frames was altogether wise, especially for the largest engines. Equalising beams were certainly not essential on British track in 1900 but they might have helped to reduce slipping by British Pacifics in the 1950s.

No 1200 of the GNR batch was sent direct to the Paris Exhibition of 1900 but there are no reports of it gaining especial honours. No 966 of the GCR was involved in a collision at Brocklesby on 27 March 1907 when it was hauling an ordinary goods train from New Holland and collided with a Grimsby-Leicester fish train worked by a 2-4-0 No 507. Driver Bollingbroke of Lincoln was held responsible for misreading signals. He received a broken leg in the accident but became regular Night Foreman at Leicester during World War I. Some of the GCR 'Yankees' were renumbered from 941-946 to 961-966 as their original numbers were wanted for some 0-6-2 tanks built in 1901. Another mishap, fortunately less serious, took place at Staveley when brake trouble on a Mogul prevented it stopping in time to avoid hitting another loose-coupled train. Happily nothing worse than bruising and shock affected both crews.

The Midland Moguls are outside the story of those on the LNER and their constituent companies, but, in as far as their reputation confirms that gained by the GNR or GCR 'Yankees', they become relevant. The American engines were not popular although the superior comfort of their cabs was appreciated. They had a reputation for needing more coal and oil than British 0-6-0s of comparable power and they were considered to be expensive to maintain. There were complaints of their rough finish but this was perhaps unfair as they were supplied very quickly and at competitive prices. They were only intended to help with secondary work. Their copper fireboxes were said to be of poorer quality than British examples. American railroad philosophy maintained that it was wiser to build an engine for a short life and then to replace it with something more modern. Some British 0-6-0s lasted longer than several generations of American freight engines. The immaculate finish given, for example, to the Johnson 0-6-0 illustrated on page 221 of E. L. Ahron's *British Steam Railway Locomotive* 1825-1925 (Locomotive Publishing Co 1927/Ian Allan, 1961) would be considered, by practical American locomotive men of the period, to be wasteful for freight engines. By 1915, barely ten years after their introduction, the last of the American Moguls had gone.

All the 2-6-0s built in the nineteenth and early twentieth centuries were intended for slow freight service and were only occasionally used on passenger services at moderate speeds. Similar work was expected of 0-6-0 engines. By the end of the first decade of the twentieth century thoughts were turning towards Moguls of a very different capability. One of G. J. Churchward's more promising young men, H. Holcroft, had visited Canada and the United States and had returned very impressed by the successful use of 2-6-0 locomotives with driving wheels just under 5 feet in diameter for all classes of traffic on some of the secondary lines. Mr Holcroft has told, in *An Outline of Great Western Practice* 1837-1947 (Ian Allan, 1957), how he suggested to his chief that a suitably designed 2-6-0 with larger driving wheels could give useful service in Britain at speeds higher than those he had observed in America. Churchward allowed him to have his way and the first of a faster type of British Mogul appeared on the GWR in 1911.

Although GWR practice lies outside the scope of this book, the success of the 4300 class Moguls had a significant influence on mixed traffic locomotive practice on several lines. The 4300s proved to be the first of a number of 2-6-0 mixed traffic designs. The Churchward Moguls were, by no means, the first 2-6-0s to appear on the GWR, but the 'Krugers' and the 'Aberdares' were only intended for heavy freight and mineral haulage. The 4300 class engines opened up an entirely new dimension of 2-6-0 capacity, proving themselves capable in emergencies of deputising for a 4-6-0 express locomotive on trains as fast as a Birmingham 2hr express or an Exeter 3hr train. Speeds in the 75-80mph range were recorded downhill thanks to the free running made possible by the combination of 5ft 8in driving wheels and the excellent valve and front end design which was the secret of Churchward's success.

The first of the Churchward 4300 class Moguls appeared in 1911 and in the following year H. N. Gresley, the newly promoted CME of the GNR, produced a 2-6-0 of similar size and capacity intended for the same duties. It might be thought that the success of the GWR type inspired the building of the GNR engines, but there could hardly have been time for the Swindon engines to have established their reputation before work on the GNR engine began. It is more likely that Gresley was thinking on similar lines to Churchward and the building of the GWR Moguls merely reinforced a policy decision already made.

11

CHAPTER TWO

The Ancestry of the First Great Northern 2-6-0 Mixed Traffic Engine

The Great Northern was mainly a long distance railway, the prizes lay at the end of the track. The main revenue came from through traffic with the North Eastern and with industrial traffic originating in the West Riding. GNR intermediate traffic was relatively light and mainly agricultural, and in this respect the GNR was in contrast to the Midland which gained considerable recenue from its intermediate stations. The late E. L. Ahrons described the GNR as being 'facile princeps' among the standard gauge railways for the speed of its trains even in the 1850s. This was no mere coincidence, the nature of the traffic gave every incentive for the GNR to hurry their trains along the road. This pattern of operation continued into modern times with the Gresley streamliners performing their fastest running over GNR metals, and it finds its present day expression in the 'Deltic' timings and faster ones proposed for the High Speed Trains.

In the very beginning railways only needed freight engines, but when the Liverpool and Manchester Railway entered business as general carriers, then faster types of engine for passenger and mail traffic had to be developed. As railways progressed it soon became obvious that more than two types of engine would be required to run a railway. A railway which needed fast passenger trains soon found that it could find profit in fast goods trains. The vast numbers of workers in the thriving factories of the nineteenth century needed to enjoy their brief periods of leisure and it was not long before the demand for cheap, popular railway travel brought the excursion train; and very soon the railways realised that something better than 'Parliamentary' travel would be required by excursion passengers. The introduction of bank holidays caused a heavy concentration of passengers over short periods.

A class of passenger traffic which some railways at first thought of as a nuisance soon became a source of revenue which could not be neglected. The Victorian era saw the rise of the popular seaside holiday and the railways assisted this tendency. The annual seaside holiday and the bank holiday day trip to the coast became a feature of life which made the lives of working people a little more tolerable. The Great Northern holiday resort most publicised was Skegness on the Lincolnshire coast, and thousands of holidaymakers were carried,

12

not only from the Midland cities of Leicester and Nottingham, but also from London. Day return tickets at 3/– a time carried travellers from Kings Cross to Skegness on bank holidays. They rode, at times, in the comfort of spare main-line corridor coaches, but more often they rode in spartan conditions in close-coupled suburban stock. The popularity of Skegness was increased by the famous GNR poster of the jolly fisherman proclaiming that 'Skegness is so bracing'. This is still regarded as one of the classic triumphs of publicity. On August Bank Holidays up to 10 specials would run between Kings Cross and the Lincolnshire coast. These all needed locomotives.

During the same period the fast goods train was becoming an increasingly important feature of all railways, but the GNR was very much the pace setter. There were meat trains coming up from Scotland, fish trains from Hull and milk trains from the Midlands, all requiring fast running over GNR metals, and trains of miscellaneous goods travelled north each day. It soon became obvious that an engine suitable for fast goods trains was also very useful at the head of an excursion train, which might well be heavier than an express but not so fast. Part of the work on both fast goods and excursion trains was performed by older express engines which had been displaced by engines larger and more modern. Even the Stirling eight-footers were used at times, either alone or in pairs, on express meat trains between Peterborough and Kings Cross. The Stirling 2-4-0s were never serious rivals to the singles on the fastest expresses and they were often used on excursion and fast goods trains, and in course of time the Ivatt 4-4-0s were used in the same way. The GNR never built a small wheeled mixed traffic 4-4-0 such as the GWR 'Bulldog'. It was soon realised that a type of engine capable of reinforcing both the express locomotives or the goods engines at times of heavy traffic was likely to be very useful.

Between 1867 and 1895 Patrick Stirling built 154 mixed traffic engines of the 0-4-2 type with only slight variations between the first and the last. The first is of historic importance in that it carried Doncaster Works No 1. Their coupled wheels were 5ft 7in in diameter and they must have been among the cheapest and simplest mixed traffic engines ever built. corresponding in their way with the LNWR 0-6-0 Webb 'Coal Engine' built for mineral traffic. The Stirling 0-4-2s ran most of the passenger traffic over the steeply graded lines of the West Riding, the greater part of the main and branch line stopping trains all over the system, much of the fast goods traffic, and they were sometimes used in pairs during the early years of the twentieth century on heavy coal or mineral trains usually hauled by Ivatt 'Long Tom' 0-8-0s. There is a persistant GNR legend that a 0-4-2 once was responsible for a valiant substitution on an express, but enquiries as to where and when bring different answers which hardly increase credibility. Old railwaymen were, however, adamant that 'A front coupler could run when it had to'. In a most interesting article in the *Journal of the Stephenson Locomotive Society*, K. H. Leech, BSc, an authority on GNR locomotives, writes that the Stirling 0-4-2 were really marvellous little engines which almost seemed to forget their limited adhesion weight when used on goods trains and their small driving wheels when used on passenger work. The value of a mixed traffic engine on the GNR was fully established by these small machines.

During Stirling's time the 0-6-0 was rarely used on passenger trains. Their rare appearances usually meant that there had been an emergency substitution. They were however strong on normal slow goods trains and used a great deal by other railways for mixed traffic work. The Johnson 'express goods' 0-6-0s of 1878 worked the Midland fast goods and wool trains between Bradford and London at an average speed of 35mph, and they also worked a large number of excursion trains. The LNWR often used the special DX and 'Cauliflower' class 0-6-0s on express trains as pilots to Webb compounds, and they have been timed at over 60mph on the level and at over 70mph down steep gradients. It is not surprising in view of what happened elsewhere that the reluctance of Stirling to use 0-6-0s on passenger trains evaporated somewhat during the Ivatt regime. Not only were the Stirling 0-6-0s then seen more often on passenger trains, but the new chief also used his own 0-6-0s frequently. There had been an upsurge in traffic during the early 1900s and recognition of the versatility of the 0-6-0 was stimulated by the need to use every available engine at holiday periods.

In 1908 H. A. Ivatt built some uncompromising mixed traffic 0-6-0s intended for fast goods and occasional passenger service. To this end he used 5ft 8in driving wheels. These were the largest driving wheels used for large scale 0-6-0 construction, though 6ft wheels were used experimentally on the Midland. The Ivatt 0-6-0s had been inspired by the success of his 0-6-2 tank engines which had similar boilers, cylinders and motion. They were used on regular fast goods and fish trains and at holiday periods on passenger trains. They were known as the 'No 1 class'. Ivatt had ideas that something larger and more powerful could be used on mixed traffic duties and in 1907 plans were drawn up for a 2-6-2, four-cylinder compound mixed-traffic engine with the Atlantic boiler. The limited success of the GNR four-cylinder compound Atlantics does not inspire much confidence in the success of this project, but the mere fact that such an engine was seriously contemplated indicates there that was the need for a large mixed traffic design.

In 1911 Mr Ivatt retired to be followed by H. N. Gresley, a relatively young man of 35. Two Ivatt designs were in production and these were carried through to completion by the new chief. The first type was a 0-6-0 superheated goods engine with 5ft 2in wheels. These later became LNER Class J6 but they were known on the GNR right into BR days as 'A Engines', which was a reference to their GNR power classification. They had Schmidt superheaters and piston valves and they could be recognised at a distance by their higher pitched boilers. The first was built in 1911 and they were added to by Gresley, forming a most useful class. They were followed in 1912 by a similar class with 5ft 8in wheels which could be regarded as superheated versions of Ivatt's No 1 class. Ten were built and put to work on the night fast goods trains to York and Manchester, while at holiday times they were used on excursion trains and even on relief portions to main line expresses. On passenger duties they were timed at up to 70mph. They were not good riding engines at such speeds and a number of former GNR enginemen preferred the smaller wheeled 5ft 2in engines for fast running, though neither class could have given a luxurious ride as speeds approached the 70mph mark.

The years leading up to World War I had seen something of a boom in fast goods traffic and not only were old express engines pressed into service but the latest Atlantics also found their way on to fast goods trains at times. The new superheated 0-6-0s were a useful reinforcement to the available motive power, but the problem was not fully solved and the first task facing Mr Gresley when he took office was that of designing a new mixed traffic engine with the adhesion weight of a 0-6-0, but which would be a better vehicle at speed. The new engine would also have to deputise for an Atlantic on all but the fastest of express trains. The 2-6-0 was the natural choice for such an engine.

Up to the end of the first decade of the twentieth century, British 2-6-0s had been small-wheeled freight engines. These could occasionally work a passenger train just as could a 0-6-0, but the regular haulage of secondary expresses or fast goods trains had never been the intention of their designers. As indicated in Chapter 1 the first Gresley 2-6-0 was built shortly after the GWR 4300 class Moguls first appeared, but there is no reason to think that Gresley was copying the Swindon design. The GNR 2-6-0 No 1630, built in 1912, was a compromise design which included enough features of traditional Doncaster design to mark its ancestry as Great Northern, but also having enough new features to serve notice that new ideas were to be expected.

CHAPTER THREE

The Two-Cylinder Gresley Moguls

The first Gresley 2-6-0 of GNR Class H2 emerged from Doncaster in August 1912.   There was no question about its basic ancestry, it was a true GNR engine with features of Ivatt and even Stirling design fully apparent externally but with the striking innovations of a raised running plate and outside Walchaerts valve gear.   It was numbered 1630.

The boiler was a development from that used on the superheated 0-6-0s but it was longer, and the additional length, made possible by the 2-6-0 wheel arrangement, had been put to good use in the shape of a larger firebox and grate area.   Superheating surface was increased and the first engines had a Schmidt type superheater.   They were fitted, as well, with superheater dampers which were eventually removed as being unnecessary.   The boiler continued the traditional GNR practice of using a round top firebox, the barrel was built in two rings and was 11ft 8in long and 4ft 8in in diameter.   The first engine had a short smokebox but this was made longer on subsequent members of the class.   The boiler pressure was a relatively moderate 170lb/sq in but this was common practice in those days for superheated engines. The boiler gained a reputation for good steaming with the high quality coal prevailing in pre-World War I conditions.   It was, however, comparatively small on the basis of Gresley's policy as established later, and an enlarged boiler was developed when the class was multiplied beyond the first ten.

The driving wheels were 5ft 8in in diameter and the leading pony truck wheels were 3ft 8in in diameter on the first engine, but this was reduced to 3ft 2in on subsequent locomotives.   The smaller wheels had more side play as the frames could be cut away to allow more lateral movement.   The first engine had frames set in at the leading end.   The pony truck was pivoted behind the cylinders and was of Gresley's patent double-bolster swing-link type, to which he adhered during his earlier years.   This had no side control springs and lubrication of the heavily loaded pins could also be a problem.   Although the H2s and all subsequent GNR and LNER Moguls were never credited with good riding qualities, there is no evidence that the swing links were the only contributing factor.   The first engine No 1630 had plate springs above the axle journals, but subsequent engines had helical coils.

The cylinders were of 20in diameter and 26in stroke with 10in piston valves above them. These valves were of the Schmidt type with a lap of 1¼in, exhaust clearance of ⅛in and a travel in full gear of 5¾in. The H2s had Trick ports which allowed an extra charge of steam which gave additional thrust to each working stroke but did nothing to help exhaust. Trick ports were used extensively on the LNWR which was noted in 1912 for superheated locomotives, especially the 'George the Fifth' class 4-4-0s, which were vigorous in performance but which had a noisy exhaust. The disadvantage was that the passages inside the valve heads became carboned up in service and the value of the extra ports became questionable as mileage mounted. Ivatt had shown considerable enthusiasm for Schmidt valves and superheaters but Gresley did not share his belief. An economy drive was in force on the GNR in 1913/14, as Gresley was contemplating the building of more 2-6-0s, and he saw no great advantage in paying royalties to the Schmidt Company when the Robinson superheater and plain ring piston valves without the Trick ports might well give equally satisfactory results. The Trick ports were not used on the 1914 engines and they were, in course of time, removed from the original ten.

The valve events of the two-cylinder GNR 2-6-0s could not be described as being of advanced design but they were better than many contemporary designs on other British railways, such as the Midland, which retained a valve travel of 3¼in on the 2-8-0s built in 1914 for the S&DJR. The use of generous exhaust clearances allowed the GNR 2-6-0s to run on short cut-offs without excessive back pressures but it was not otherwise a desirable feature for efficiency. In those days locomotive engineers believed that it was easier to get steam into the cylinders than out, but with the coming of long travel valves the reverse was nearer to the truth at short cut-offs, and modern engines suffered from inlet throttling. In this respect a return to the Trick ports might have been considered along the lines of the French Willoteaux pattern. The basic pattern of the GNR cylinders was used, with only minor changes, for the B1 class 4-6-0s cylinder casting, but of course with long travel valves. The B1s gave excellent cylinder performance on the Rugby Plant.

The cylinders were fitted with piston tail rods when new but they were removed later. Steam sanding was used on the driving wheels and gravity sanding before the front pair and behind the rear pair of coupled axles. The axlebox journals were 8½in dia × 10in long, the hornblocks were of the simple horseshoe type with adjustable wedges. The cylinders were lubricated by a Wakefield mechanical lubricator with the firm's anti-carbonising device. The cab was of traditional GNR design with round spectacle glasses in front; it was rather spartan giving limited comfort and protection for the crew. The Stirling type of pull-out regulator and lever reverse were retained. The standard GNR 3,500 gallon tender with water pick up and capacity for 6½ tons of coal was used.

As first built, the 10 engines filled the need for a fast goods engine and they promised to be better than 0-6-0s or ageing express locomotives on such work. A test run was carried out with the borrowed GWR dynamometer car and 57 box vans. No 1630 was first sent to London and was seen on semi-fast outer suburban trains as well as on seasonal excursion work. They took over the work of the large boilered 0-6-0s on the night fast goods to Manchester and York. The late F. H. Gillford photographed them at outposts such as Derby Friargate quite early in their careers.

Compared with the standards established later by Gresley, the 4ft 8in diameter boiler was small for 20in × 26in cylinders and it is not surprising that this was altered in the next batch built in 1914. These had boilers 5ft 6in in diameter with the Robinson superheater. Ivatt had used the Schmidt superheater and valves but Gresley did not relish the continuation and escalation of royalty payments. The Robinson superheater proved to be perfectly satisfactory and it was later standardised by Gresley for the LNER. The elements were expanded directly into the header and they gave no trouble. A problem which worried locomotive engineers in the early days of superheating was the alleged burning of superheater elements when the regulator was closed and many devices were designed to alleviate this and the associated problem of hot oil carbonising in the cylinders. As with many valuable inventions the superheater brought difficulties as well as benefits and Churchward's use of low superheat only was not without merit.

The first Gresley 2-6-0s had superheater dampers which were eventually removed as unnecessary. The larger 1914 batch had a small snifting valve similar to Ivatt's pattern but these proved too small. On his later three-cylinder 2-6-0s Gresley introduced his larger anti-vacuum or snifting valve which allowed cold air to be drawn through the superheater into the cylinders and this later became standard. On the SR Maunsell fitted a similar valve and S. C. Townroe has described some SR tests that suggested that the snifting valve was unnecessary. The presence of hot air in the cylinders would tend to exacerbate the carbonisation problem. It would appear that the problem of ashes down the blast pipe, though seemingly fatal, was in fact more apparent than real and may even have helped to keep the valves clean.

Grate and ashpan arrangements.

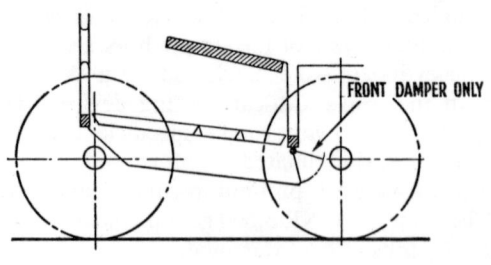

FRONT DAMPER ONLY

K1 (GNR) AND K2

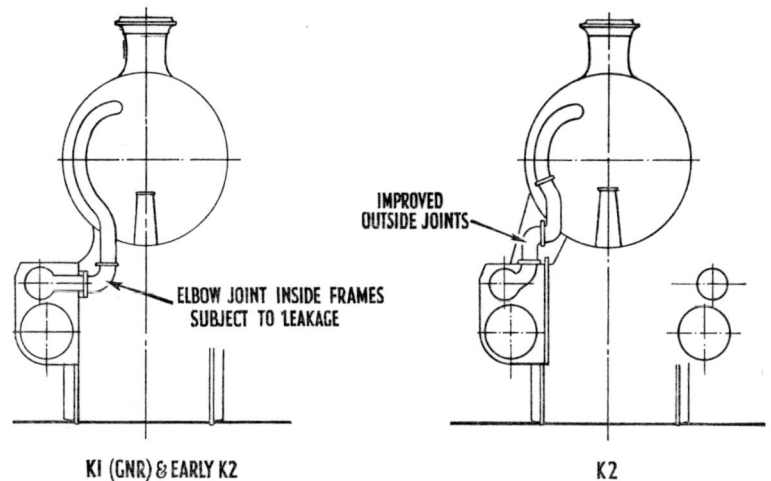

IMPROVED
OUTSIDE JOINTS

ELBOW JOINT INSIDE FRAMES
SUBJECT TO LEAKAGE

KI (GNR) & EARLY K2   K2

Steam pipe arrangements.

The firebox remained unaltered. The larger boiler improved the appearance of the engines and there was better sustained performance though starting ability was not affected. Gresley claimed that the larger engines had a coal consumption lower by 5lb per mile.

The Trick ports and Schmidt piston valve rings were abandoned with the superheater changes but the valve events remained the same with a maximum travel of $5\frac{3}{4}$in. The cab had to be modified to fit the larger boiler and shaped front windows replaced the round ones of the earlier engines. There were larger lightening holes cut in the main frames to counteract the increased weight of the larger boiler and the increase in total weight was kept to under three tons. The slide bars were shortened and a motion plate of different shape was moved forward to a position in front of the expansion link. In later years, when the 10 originals had all received the larger boiler, the difference in slide bars and motion plate remained. The new engines were 8ft 11in, instead of 8ft 7in, between pony wheels and first set of drivers.

Doncaster built 10 H3s in 1914; they were numbered 1640-1649 and another 10, Nos 1650-1659, followed in 1916. The first 10 were painted GNR green, as were the first two of the second batch, but the remainder were painted in shop grey which the GNR adopted for secondary locomotives during the wartime emergency. The first 10 had the smaller axleboxes as used on Nos 1630-1639, but subsequent engines had larger, standard $9\frac{1}{2}$in × 11in axleboxes as used on the Pacifics. In LNER days the GNR H2s became LNER Class K1, those H3s with the smaller axleboxes became LNER Class K2/1, and those from 1650 onwards with the larger axleboxes became K2/2.

An early trouble with the first K1s and K2s was leakage from the main inside steam pipes between the smokebox and the cylinders.

19

This was formed by a short right-angled elbow piece which was very inaccessible and difficult to keep steam tight. In 1915 20 2-6-0s were ordered from Beyer Peacock at a price of £3,800 apiece but the pressure of war work made them unable to carry it out and they were finished by the North British Loco Co at an increased price in 1917. Those built by Kitsons after the war, in 1921, cost £9,880 but prices fell by the 1930s and the last K3 built in 1937 cost £5,455. The engines delivered in 1917 from the NBL Co had outside steam pipes housed in square casings and the leakage problem was solved. In course of time those built with inside steam pipes had them replaced as they came in for recylindering. In some cases the cylinder on one side needed renewing earlier than that on the other and then a dummy steam pipe was fitted. It is understood that one engine was turned out from Cowlairs without a dummy steam pipe casing on one side and it ran for some time with this unbalanced appearance, though of course nothing really fundamental was affected.

The engines from the North British Loco Co were delivered in shop grey and the last of the batch was built in 1919 bringing the class up to No 1679. A final batch Nos 1680-1704 was built by Kitson and Co in 1921 and these were delivered in GNR green. The piston tail rods disappeared in this batch and in course of time they were removed from other earlier engines. The original K1s had one mechanical lubricator for the cylinders and steam chests and a second lubricator was added later for the axleboxes. The Doncaster built K2s had two mechanical lubricators. The North British batch had hydrostatic lubrication fed by a Detroit sight feed lubricator in the cab for the cylinders and valves, with a mechanical lubricator for the axleboxes. The Kitson engines had a similar system but had the Detroit sight feed lubricator on the opposite side of the cab. Some of the Detroits were still in use in the 1950s but the view finally prevailed that lubrication should not be under the control of the driver. The hydrostatic system was basically a simple one and it was used on the 1943 Austerity 2-8-0s while the GWR had a similar system which apparently gave every satisfaction. No final decision between the sight feed and the purely mechanical types was ever clearly established and it remained one of the unresolved issues of steam practice.

The original K2s were only allowed on lines with a generous height allowance and when it was thought that some could be used on the GER and in Scotland they had to be reduced in height. This meant shorter chimneys and domes and the removal of the whistle from the cab roof, which was lowered by 3in. There were, once again, individual variations and a photograph exists of 4657 with a short chimney but retaining the larger K1 type dome and with its whistle still on the cab roof. In 1925 14 K2s were transferred to the West Highland line in Scotland. Another six followed in 1931/2 for use on the eastern side of the country from Edinburgh or Thornton. The West Highland engines allowed passenger train loading to be increased to 220 tons but the 2-6-0s were not enthusiastically received from the point of view of cab comfort and between 1932 and 1935 all the Scottish area K2s were given side window cabs. The new cabs were not all fitted at once and a photograph exists of No 4692 *Loch Eil* still retaining its GNR type cab, though with glass deflector screens. In 1934 the 13 engines regularly working on the West Highland all received the names of Scottish lochs. Their Scottish connection led to the whole class being sent to Cowlairs for overhaul and this brought about the painting of the shed name on the buffer beam even after LMS style shed plates were fitted in BR days.

The cutting down in height of K2 class engines to fit them for more general use was not welcomed by GNR enginemen who said that steaming was adversely affected. In this connection it is interesting to note that Atlantic No 1447 was cut down in a similar way to allow it to take part in comparative running over the NER and NBR in 1923, and the coal consumption of the GNR engine was the highest of all the Atlantics tested. No 4447 in later LNER days was never considered to be a very good steamer but the booster fitted Atlantic No 4419, which was similarly treated, was quite a flyer in the Kings Cross Pullman link when handled by Driver Charlie Barnes.

A number of detailed modifications were made to individual engines. In 1921 six K2s Nos 1641/67/8/9/71/4 were fitted with the Scarab system of oil firing during the coal strike, but only limited success was reported. Those engines transferred to the GER were cut down in height and fitted with a Westinghouse brake pump mounted on the right hand side in front of the cab. The engines sent to the West Highland were fitted with deeper ashpans for the lower quality Scottish coal, as the standard GNR type latterly became blocked solid with ash. The GNR-built engines and those from the NBL Co were fitted with four Ramsbottom safety valves in a typical GNR casing. The Kitson-built engines had two 'pop' valves and all of the class received these eventually. Those engines used on the M&GNJR were fitted with tablet catchers.

The worst fault of the engines was their rough riding which gained them the nickname of 'Ragtimers' quite early in their careers. As with most rough engines their riding could be improved by good maintenance and attention to the axleboxes and Driver J. Storr of Boston shed recalls good trips with loads of 12-15 bogies on excursion trains. The lever reverse was unpopular and it needed steam off and, at times, both men to move it. It was only kept in position by the vacuum lock or it would slip into full gear. The engines were not driven on the cut-off, the best results were obtained with around 30 per cent cut-off with the second regulator used during acceleration, changing over to the first for continuous running. Much longer cut-offs were needed on the West Highland banks but the valve setting proved quite good for this slogging. They were not the aristocrats of the steam age but they did a useful job for their owners.

CHAPTER FOUR

The K3 Class Moguls

The Gresley GNR Class H4, LNER Class K3, 2-6-0s arose out of the 1918 proposal of the Association of Railway Locomotive Engineers, which was given the task of preparing a range of standard types for use on all railways.   The GWR CME, George Jackson Churchward, was the chairman and it has been said that he was regarded with great respect by the participating engineers from other railways.   The main design work for the standard types however, was undertaken by Maunsell from the SE&CR and Fowler from the Midland.   The outline drawings, which have survived, were made at Derby and it is interesting to speculate on whether the forward looking policy of Ashford, which accepted Churchward's long lap and long travel valves, would have prevailed in face of the reactionary forces at Derby who were destined later to delay the adoption of enlightened front end design on the LMS.   The proposed 2-6-0 would have been larger than Gresley two-cylinder Moguls but smaller than the 2-6-0 he had in mind.   Gresley appears to have had no great enthusiasm for standard designs not of GNR origin and requiring different spare parts.

The Government wanted to reduce unemployment by building locomotives at Woolwich Arsenal in 1919/1920 and as the drawings were not ready for large scale production of the standard 2-6-0, the existing SECR Class N Mogul was substituted.   Some of these 2-6-0s, slightly smaller than the proposed standard design, might very easily have run on LNER lines as the Great Eastern seriously considered ordering 20 or 30 in 1920, but, as these could not be delivered as quickly as was desired, the order was cancelled.   The Woolwich project is described in full in *The Maunsell Moguls* by P. Rowledge (Oakwood Press, 1976).

Some indication of the ideas in Gresley's mind is shown by a line drawing of a 2-6-2 tank engine proposed in 1919 and developed into a 2-6-4T in the following year.   Now a 2-6-2T or 2-6-4T could just as easily be built as a 2-6-0 tender engine.   The drawings in *Nigel Gresley Locomotive Engineer*, by F. A. S. Brown (Ian Allan, 1961) show the tank engines with very short chimneys, but that was to allow them to reach Moorgate; their boilers were no larger than those of the two-cylinder Moguls of GN Class H3 later to be LNER Class K2.   Three-cylinders and 5ft 8in driving wheels with a larger boiler first appeared in a 2-6-0 in March 1920 forming the prototype of LNER Class K3.

The idea of a large mixed traffic engine had been a feature of GNR thinking for many years and this need had not been filled by the two-cylinder 2-6-0s. In 1907 Ivatt had made preliminary designs for a four-cylinder compound 2-6-2 with 5ft 8in driving wheels and in 1915 Gresley prepared designs for two four-cylinder simple express passenger Pacifics with either a wide or a narrow firebox. These were based on the experimental rebuilding of Atlantic No 279 with four cylinders. In 1918, following the building of the experimental three-cylinder 2-8-0 No 461, Gresley decided that the three-cylinder simple engine promised more for future GNR practice. In 1918 designs were prepared for 2-6-2 three-cylinder express engines and by 1920 these had developed into a Pacific. Rumours of these projects had leaked out and when the large three-cylinder 2-6-0 No 1000 appeared in March 1920, Cecil J. Allen referred to disappointment that this was not the expected 2-6-2 or 4-6-2. GNR enthusiasts had to wait until 1922 for their large express engine, but with hindsight it can be claimed that in some important aspects of design the 2-6-0 of 1920 was the more advanced machine.

By the standards of 1920 the first GNR three-cylinder Mogul was in many respects a landmark in locomotive development. It was the first British locomotive with a boiler of 6ft diameter, and it was this short fat boiler which first caught the eye and stimulated the imagination of a 1920 lineside observer. The large boiler meant a chimney short by GNR standards, and a seven-year old boy, destined later to become one of the writers of this book, thought of his coloured postcard of a North British Atlantic as the smokebox front of No 1006 came into sight at Grantham. The boiler barrels were formed from a single plate of steel with a longitudinal joint. The boiler, with its 28sq ft of grate area, had ample steaming capacity to make effective the tractive effort of 30,000lb. The free gas area through the tubes was 19 per cent of the grate area which was well in excess of the 15 per cent which might have been considered to be adequate. The grate area could possibly have been larger to take more advantage of the 6ft diameter boiler.

An alternative modification might have been to have used a boiler of smaller diameter, possibly 5ft 9in, which would have retained an

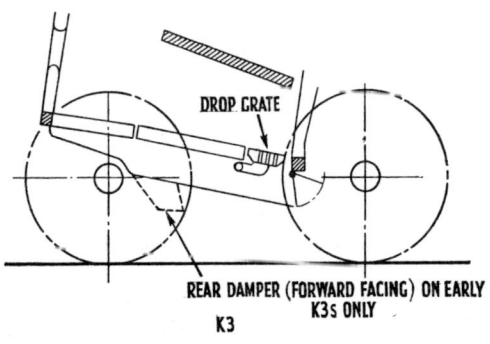

DROP GRATE

REAR DAMPER (FORWARD FACING) ON EARLY
K3s ONLY

K3

acceptable percentage of free gas area and would have permitted a lighter engine with a wider route availability. Gresley, however, claimed that considerable economy had resulted from the enlarged boiler on the two-cylinder Moguls. The extra steam space and water capacity of the large diameter boiler provided valuable thermal storage capacity and Gresley once said that he would rather carry an extra ton of hot water about than add more weight to the frames to increase adhesion. Those same design features which militated against a wide route availability were an asset for heavy long-distance main-line work. Gresley was also strongly in favour of the large diameter round top boiler in preference to the Belpaire type, which was popular elsewhere, but which Doncaster considered to be more costly and heavier for a given size.

The GNR 1000 class 2-6-0s had a 32-element Robinson superheater with a heating surface of 407sq ft. This was a large superheater for the size of the boiler and footplate observers reported steam temperatures of 650-700F°. The fireboxes were originally fitted with front and back dampers, but in the early 1930s experiments showed that, with improved draughting, they steamed just as well with the rear one closed and burnt less coal. Commencing in August 1932 with No 1158 they were built with front dampers only. Older enginemen do not all accept the official verdict and some consider that the engines were less effective after the change.

The Gresley anti-vacuum or snifting valve was fitted; this allowed cold air to be drawn through the superheater and into the cylinders and it later became LNER standard equipment. Opinion was divided as to whether these valves were wholly beneficial. They occasionally gave trouble with jamming and chattering. Corrosion was a problem and bronze valves were fitted to some engines in 1946. The presence of air may well have been essential to the formation of carbon and it probably exacerbated the problem. Carbonisation was a disadvantage which accompanied high steam temperatures and it provided some justification for Churchward's policy of low superheat.

No 1000 was the first engine to have the later form of conjugate valve motion with horizontal arms in front of the cylinders. This was a much simpler arrangement than that used by Gresley on 2-8-0 No 461 and the original inspiration came from H. Holcroft of the SE&CR whose ideas for a simplified form of conjugate gear were presented in a letter to *The Engineer* in August 1918, followed by a paper to the Institution of Locomotive Engineers. Gresley was impressed by the simplicity of Holcroft's gear and decided to adopt it.

As first fitted to No 1000, the maximum cut-off was 75 per cent with 6⅜in valve travel and 1½in lap. This was an enlightened design but subsequent events suggest that its merit was not fully appreciated. The first two engines had early trouble due to inertia forces and over running of the centre valve. This influenced the choice of short lap valves for the first Pacific in 1922. The main lever was of light con-

Diagram of Class K3 showing Davis and Metcalf steam feed heating system and rear firebox damper fitted to early engines only. Superheater header and elements omitted for greater simplicity.

Water Level

Exhaust Steam

Grease Separator

Injector

struction with lightening holes and it suffered from whip. This was modified to a stiffer box construction. The fulcrum attachment also broke loose and stiffer bolts had to be fitted. Maximum cut-off in full gear was reduced from 75 to 65 per cent and was later standardised for all Gresley three-cylinder engines. The main pivot points were provided with ball bearings but during World War II supplies of these were restricted and plain bearings had to be substituted. This, combined with lower standards of maintenance, contributed to the disrepute into which the K3s sank and it provided ammunition for the Thompson two-cylinder rebuilding policy.

The valve and front end design of the 1000 class was advanced for 1920 and any troubles that this caused at first were overcome without sacrificing their free running qualities. With hindsight it seems a retrograde step when Doncaster reacted to the ring breakages of the centre valve on the 2-6-0s by retaining short lap, short travel valves on the first Pacifics. Had the valves of the K3s been used on the Pacifics there would have been no humiliation at the hands of *Pendennis Castle* in 1925. There would however have remained one advantage to the K3s, in that an 8in diameter valve was large for an 18½in-cylinder, while there was no room for the location of anything larger with the 20in-cylinders of the Pacifics. It was only with the A4s and V2s which combined a 9in diameter valve with 18½in-cylinders that further progress was made. The early K3s had a ¼in exhaust clearance with ⅛in lead and 1¼in lap which made them very free running, but later it was found that the exhaust clearance, or negative lap, was unnecessary with leads as short as ⅛in and the valves were given a line and line exhaust setting with a slight increase in lap to 1⅝in. The K3s had a greater potential for short cut-off working and their maximum speed capacity was limited more by their riding qualities than by their capacity for high rotational speeds.

A standard GNR type cab, slightly longer than that on the Atlantics, was adopted. There were twin regulator handles, one on each side of the cab, which replaced the pull-out type on the two-cylinder 2-6-0s which had originated with Patrick Stirling. A vertical screw reverser was fitted with vacuum lock and a cut-off scale on the firebox front. The view ahead was very good for an engine with a 6ft diameter boiler. The tender was of the standard GNR 3,500 gallon type as used in the K1s and K2s.

The cylinder layout was destined to be followed in a number of later Gresley designs. The outside cylinders were inclined at 1 in 30 and the inside cylinder drove on the same middle axle and was inclined at 1 in 8½. The piston valves were 8in in diameter and were above the outside cylinders and alongside the inside cylinder. The three piston valves were in the same transverse plane and the angled inside cylinder was fed by inclined ports. This was the Holcroft suggestion which made the simplified conjugated motion possible. The inclined inside cylinder was necessary to clear the leading coupled axle. Gresley, and

26

later Bulleid, always preferred this arrangement for their cylinders, instead of the divided drive as used on the 'Royal Scots'. Gresley only accepted divided drive with reluctance on the B17 class 4-6-0s built by the N.B. Loco Co.

Walschaert's valve gear was used on the two outside piston valves with Skefko ball bearings on the return crank pin. The slide bars and light crosshead were the first examples of the three-bar type which was to be used on subsequent Gresley outside cylindered engines and which was later made standard for BR designs. This layout took up little space and gave excellent protection from dust and dirt to the sliding surfaces. The motion was made as light as possible by using alloy steel rods machined down to the minimum safe thickness. The rods were 35 per cent lighter than the corresponding parts of the K2 Moguls. The large holes in the main frames, as used on the later K2s, were adopted to reduce weight. Although the weight of No 1000 was not excessive for an engine of such power, it was still the heaviest engine on eight wheels and the axle loading of 20 tons per coupled axle limited their route availability. The adhesion factor of 4.5, however, made them good starters and they showed considerable superiority to the Atlantics when used on exceptionally heavy passengers trains.

Ten engines were built by the GNR in 1920, Nos 1000-1009, and they soon proved their worth in the 1921 coal strike. Following the grouping of the railways in 1923 Gresley was appointed CME of the LNER and in 1924 more K3s were built at Darlington. These were built to the loading gauge suitable for the northern sections of the LNER which were more restricted than the GNR. The total height was reduced from 13ft 4in to 13ft 0in and the chimney, which had seemed small on the GNR engines, was made shorter still. The Darlington-built engines had a distinctly NER appearance despite their GNR origin. The cab was similar to that on the NER B16 class 4-6-0s with side windows set quite low on the cab sides. The 'enlarged' cab was an illusion as the boiler projected further into the cab space leaving the crew with no more room. The Group Standard tender, which was developed at Darlington and followed the general appearance of NER design, added to the impression. Some of the Darlington built K3s, Nos 202-231, had steam reversers which proved to be less suitable for short cut-off working than the Gresley pattern. It was a little surprising that these engines were allocated to the Southern area where they became less popular. The steam reversers were removed in 1931 and fitted to T1 class 4-8-0 tanks which, by nature of their shunting duties, needed them more than main line mixed traffic engines.

More K3s were built at Doncaster in 1929 and these were the first to have the longer lap of 1⅝in. The cab windows followed the pattern of the Pacifics and the tops were raised closer to the roof. As the Darlington-built K3s went to their next Work's repair they were altered to this pattern and in 1939 the original 10 with plain GNR cabs were brought into line. The top handrail was moved to the front of the cab on the Doncaster engines. The 1929 batch had Group Standard tenders but these had flush sides and a new standard LNER style evolved, not immediately recognisable as NER or GNR. Further batches followed, as detailed in the Engine Summary, from Darlington and from outside builders. In the depression of 1932 an order for five to be built at Darlington was cancelled and they were subsequently built in 1934 by Robert Stephenson's, while an order for 10 cancelled at Darlington were later built by Armstrong Whitworth's. The last K3 No 3832 was completed at Darlington in February 1937 making a total of 193 engines. There would have been one more, No 3833, but the order for the final batch was amended from 25 to 24 and the last engine was replaced by the first K4 for the West Highland, No 3441. A note issued on 23 September 1936 gave priority of construction to No 3441 which was actually finished before the last K3. Further building of large mixed traffic engines was limited to the 2-6-2 V2 class.

There were six part numbers in the K3 classification, mainly affecting weight distribution, springing, and tender sizes. There were some interchanges of tender and the general picture is given in the appendices. The K3s had a more restricted route availability than the Gresley A1 type Pacifics; the A1s were RA7 while the K3s were RA8. They shared RA8 with the NER rebuilt B16/2s and B16/3s of roughly similar power, but the original NER B16/1s and the GCR B7s were RA7. The more powerful 2-6-2 V2s were RA9. The restricted route availability was a legitimate point of criticism of the K3 and Gresley accepted the need for a mixed traffic engine of similar power with a wider range of action when he designed the V4 class 2-6-2s which with RA4 could run almost anywhere. The Thompson B1 4-6-0s were RA5.

The first two K3s Nos 1000/1 had mechanical lubricators with friction drive but sight feed lubricators were used on the remainder of the first batch. Some drivers felt that the sight feed lubricators under their control were better; this was in accord with Swindon practice. On later LNER K3s the Wakefield mechanical lubricator with atomisers became standard. The LNER was constantly striving for improvements to reduce the incidence of hot boxes and an improved bearing material known as 'White bronze' was adopted together with a special lubricant containing 15 per cent rape oil known as 'W' oil. This was successful and was later used on the LMS Class 4 0-6-0s which were giving trouble during World War II.

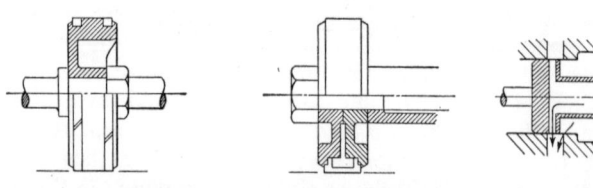

TWO NARROW SPLIT RINGS (EARLY K3s)   GRESLEY PLAIN BROAD RING VALVE (K2s & EARLY PACIFICS)   TRICK PORTED VALVE (GNR K1s)

Steam Port shapes.

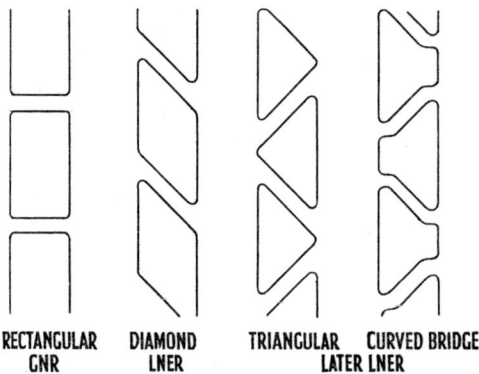

| RECTANGULAR | DIAMOND | TRIANGULAR | CURVED BRIDGE |
| GNR | LNER | LATER | LNER |

At the time when No 1000 was first built, the problems of piston valve lubrication with high temperature steam were worrying locomotive engineers and Gresley was aiming at exceptionally high temperatures. There was much development and variation of valve design on the K3s. A parallel story of trial and error on the LMS is described by E. S. Cox in *Locomotive Panorama, Vol. 1;* Ian Allan, 1965.

The first K3s on the GNR had a split-ring valve with two narrow rings somewhat similar to that used on the Pennsylvania RR but without their hollow trunk feature. The rings themselves formed the cut-off edges of the valve, which was, in itself, a good feature, but they tended to wear the bridges of the liner ports which were of rectangular shape and ring seizures and breakages occurred. On his Pacifics Gresley returned to broad ring valves, perfectly plain without grooves of any kind. As is well known, these were neither successful on the LNER nor elsewhere. Successive trials were made on the K3s built at Darlington in 1924/5 with both broad and narrow rings. Nos 17-73 Broad ring, 75-120 Narrow ring, 121-158 Narrow ring, 159-200 Broad ring, 202-231 Narrow ring.

Trouble persisted and at this stage the broad ring was still in favour due mainly to its more even liner wear, but there was considerable leakage and deterioration of performance with mileage. About 1927 a liner with diagonal ports was introduced which evened out the wear on the ports and rings, enabling the narrow ring to be used more successfully. These later valves had four narrow rings ⅜in wide. A further problem was that the cut-off edges then became indistinct when set to the valve head especially after heavy carbonisation. Aluminium alloy valves heads were tried at about the same time and a hollow trunk valve to improve exhaust flow similar to Pennsylvania RR practice.

A final solution was adopted in 1932 and that was to use ring controlled cut-off valves with four narrow rings but with the valve head turned down to give sharp steam edges. This valve remained the LNER standard till the end but there was a further refinement with the introduction of a curved port bridge to give better port openings.

All this time the long versus short valve travel battle was raging at Doncaster and Derby while Ashford had already been converted to Swindon practice. The long travel valve was held by some to have exacerbated the problems of wear and leakage and these considerations may excuse in part Gresley's reluctance to adopt the long travel at first. There was much debate in professional circles over valve design and locomotive men on other railways must have looked with some wistful envy at Swindon, who could afford to stay aloof from such discussions as they did not use high temperature steam and so largely avoided the carbonisation problems which were never fully solved with high superheat. Swindon of course had to face similar problems when they adopted high superheat after World War II.

The K3s built from 1929 onwards had the slightly longer lap of $1\frac{5}{8}$in as on the modified Pacifics. Some LNER engineers considered that the success of narrow rings had done as much for coal consumption as long travel and it is very difficult to judge the truth of this claim. Since both narrow rings and long travel were both introduced at the same time the effect of one masked that of the other modification to some extent.

There were few modifications to K3s which were externally apparent but in 1936 No 227 was fitted with an electrical foam detector to give warning of priming. There were other less obvious modifications; Wakefield mechanical lubricators with anti carbonisation valves were fitted from 1929 onwards; diamond soot blowers were tried on Nos 2761-2766; roller bearings were fitted throughout the valve gear of the batch built in 1934 in an attempt to improve the irregularities of the 2 and 1 gear, but later this was found to be unnecessary and was removed. Modifications were made to the gudgeon pin lubrication in 1935 and this was made retrospective on all Gresley three-cylinder classes. It was thought that heavy wear of the small end of the inside inclined connecting rod, due to inadequate lubrication, had contributed to big end failures. Also from 1935 lagging covers were fitted over the cylinder exhaust passages as the hot parts could be a hazard to crews.

Following some trials intended for the Pacifics, K3 No 109 was

Valve rings.

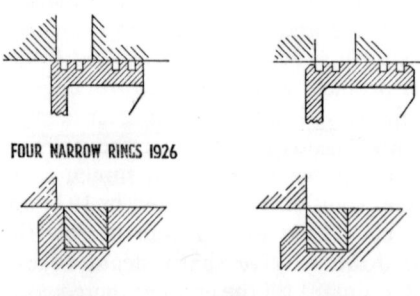

FOUR NARROW RINGS 1926

HEAD CONTROL

RING CONTROLLED VALVE, STANDARD FROM 1932

fitted with Michell-type tilting pad bearings to give an improved oil film thickness at the journal. This was a promising development which might have reduced the incidence of hot boxes but it required considerable alteration to the axleboxes and it was not perpetuated. Michell type bearings had been widely used for high speed turbines. Following redraughting trials, conducted by the Southern area running department, the K3s built from 1929 onwards had blastpipes set 4in lower and with nozzle diameter increased from 5in to 5⅜in. Existing engines were modified as they passed through the shops.

The minimum mileage laid down in 1932 for a K3 between general repairs was 50,000 for the Southern and Scottish areas and 65,000 for the NE area. In 1947 this was changed to 60,000 for all engines. The last K3 cost £3,136 for the engine, £1,273 for the boiler and £1,046 for the tender, making a total of £5,455.

Up to the outbreak of war the K3 class had a good general reputation. Those Kings Cross and New England engines intended for the best work such as the down 15.40 'Scotch Goods' were maintained in a condition worthy of an express engine, but by 1939 the V2s were taking over such tasks and the K3 were dropping in status. Before the war some splendid performances were made by Doncaster men working over the GCR on express goods and, at times, on passenger workings such as the Penzance-Aberdeen. Two or three of the Annesley engines were given first class treatment and responded accordingly, while the Immingham engines were considered to be very reliable being fed with 'Graphited' oil to their axleboxes. There were some rough examples at Woodford but their crews got good work from them.

During the war and for a considerable time after, they were in terrible condition, but later some individual engines improved. Some of the best were at Lowestoft for the fish traffic while some March engines were better than the average, but the general reputation of the class never recovered to the pre-war level of esteem.

The lot of footplate crews on K3s was never an easy one. There were exceptions but most deserved their nickname of the 'Jazzers'. The side window cabs gave better shelter from the weather than the GNR type at first on the original 10 but later some men preferred the GN cabs because the side window type rattled much more; the windows soon got loose and various devices were used to peg them to reduce noise. During the war glass was replaced by sheet tin which made more noise than ever and a former GCR driver recalls a spell of 14 hours wartime duty on a K3 with no side protection at all. The three types of cab seats were all criticised, the 'piano stool' type being particularly unpopular.

During the later years of the war the Thompson policy of using two cylinders where possible, instead of three, was in full swing and No 206 was fitted with a Diagram 96A boiler working at 225lb/sq in. Similar boilers, reduced in pressure to 180lb, were used on 35 K3s. The firebox wrapper plates were thinner than those on the standard K3s. A Schmidt superheater replaced the Robinson pattern. The higher pressure allowed a tractive effort of 29,250lb to be obtained from two cylinders 20in × 26in. The leading pony truck had side control springs instead of swing links and it had plate springs above the axleboxes instead of the normal K2 or K3 type helical springs. This was a reversion to the design of the original GNR 2-6-0 No 1630. On one occasion the springs collapsed and the engine was got home by using wooden rail chocks to support the front end. The twin Gresley pull-out regulator handles were replaced by a Thompson type single handle, working across the firebox back-plate. The front portion of the frame was raised higher than that of a K3 over the cylinders, making an easy visual identification feature.

The rebuilt No 206 was classified K5 and was first put into traffic in June 1945; it was renumbered 1863 in 1946 and was withdrawn as BR No 61863 in June 1960. No more K3s were rebuilt as K5s which suggests something short of the desired success attended this rebuilding. It is alleged that it needed more attention to the framing at each works visit on account of its increased shouldering tendency. This was apparent to the lineside observer when the engine was in motion. It was easily identified audibly at a distance, as the crisp, even exhaust, similar to that of a B1, was in contrast to the irregular muffled beat of a run down K3.

In 1946 trials were held between the rebuilt K5 and a standard K3 between New England and Ferme Park on loaded freight trains returning with the empties. The first set of trials took place in January at the same time that the K1/1 was being tested. It was recommended that a further set of trials should be made in September 1946 after No 206 had run 50,000 miles, but by then the K3 used in January had only run 42,000 miles and another which had a more representative mileage of 50,000 was also used. These were merely coal consumption trials, no dynamometer car was used and coal/dbhp/hr figures were not obtained. Trials of a similar nature were held between Gresley and Thompson Pacifics, between the three-cylinder B17s and the two-cylinder rebuild of Class B2, and between the rebuilt K1/1 and a J39 class 0-6-0. Although coal/mile and coal/ton mile figures are of limited significance and are of less value than dynamometer car recordings, some reliable general conclusions emerge.

New England-Ferme Park, January 1946
Load 719 tons up, 423 tons down.   Coal: Harworth Grade 1.

Engine	lb/ton mile	lb/mile
K5 No 206	.105	58.6
	.100	54.7
	.101	57.8
K3 No 2425	.105	59.9
	.116	62.9

K3 No 61830 climbs to Stanway Summit near Colchester with a up stopping train from Clacton. *P. M. Alexander*

Top left: The first British 2-6-0 GER No 527 built by Neilson in 1879 for Massey Bromley; showing sandbox on boiler, spoke balance weights and handrails on tender.   *Locomotive Publishing Co*

Centre left: GNR American built 2-6-0 No 1183 with safety valves on dome and whistle stand over firebox.   Built by Baldwin in 1899.   *Ian Allan Library*

Bottom left: The GCR version of American 2-6-0 with safety valves over firebox and Parker chimney.   The bar frames are visible in this photograph.   Built 1900.   *Ian Allan Library*

Top: The first Gresley 2-6-0 GNR No 1630 of 1912.   No 1630 had larger pony wheels and a shorter smokebox than subsequent engines.   GNR Class H2, LNER Class K1.   *Locomotive Publishing Co*

Above: GNR No 1636 a production example of Class H2 built 1913 with the longer smokebox and small pony wheels.   The smokebox damper seen on No 1630 had already been removed on No 1636 shown in GNR wartime grey livery.   *J. Cliffe Collection*

Top: GNR H2 No 1638 approaching Radcliffe-on-Trent with a Derby-Grantham stopping train c1920. *L&GRP No 16459*

Above: No 4630 as LNER Class K1 still with small boiler but with shorter chimney at Colwick c1928. *T. G. Hepburn*

Top right: K1 No 4638 in original condition with inside steam pipes at Grantham c1925. *T. G. Hepburn*

Centre right: No 4638 still as K1 but with outside steam pipes and later style LNER livery at Grantham c1930. *T. G. Hepburn*

Bottom right: K1 No 4639 with cut down chimney at Colwick c1928. *T. G. Hepburn*

Below: No 1635 as rebuilt with larger boiler to GNR Class H3 LNER Class K2. Seen at Nottingham Victoria c1922. *T. G. Hepburn*

Bottom: GNR Class H3 2-6-0 No 1641 fitted for oil burning on a down train near New Barnet 1921. *H. Gordon Tidey*

Top right: K2 No 1685N in first LNER livery with suffix N at Doncaster in 1924. *T. G. Hepburn*

Centre right: No 4631 rebuilt to Class K2 in second style livery with smaller composite gauge chimney and inside steam pipes taking water at Grantham c1930. *T. G. Hepburn*

Bottom right: K2 No 4692 as first sent to Scotland in 1925. One of the later Kitson batch with Hydrostatic lubricators, pop valves and outside steam pipes. Piston tail rods have been removed. *T. G. Hepburn*

Top: K2 No 4659 at Nottingham Victoria.   Built Doncaster 1916 with mechanical lubrication.   Shown with cut down chimney but retaining original dome, rebuilt with outside steam pipes.   *T. G. Hepburn*

Above: K2 No 4657 at Peterborough with K1 dome but with cut down chimney.   It retains inside steam pipes.   *T. G. Hepburn*

Top right: K2 No 4692 *Loch Eil* with smaller Cowlairs tender lettering but retaining GNR cab.   *T. G. Hepburn*

Centre right: K2 No 1732 in postwar LNER green shunting at Nottingham Victoria in 1948.   *T. G. Hepburn*

Bottom right: K2 No 61764 with side window cab at Fort William on 26 May 1957.   *R. F. Orpwood*

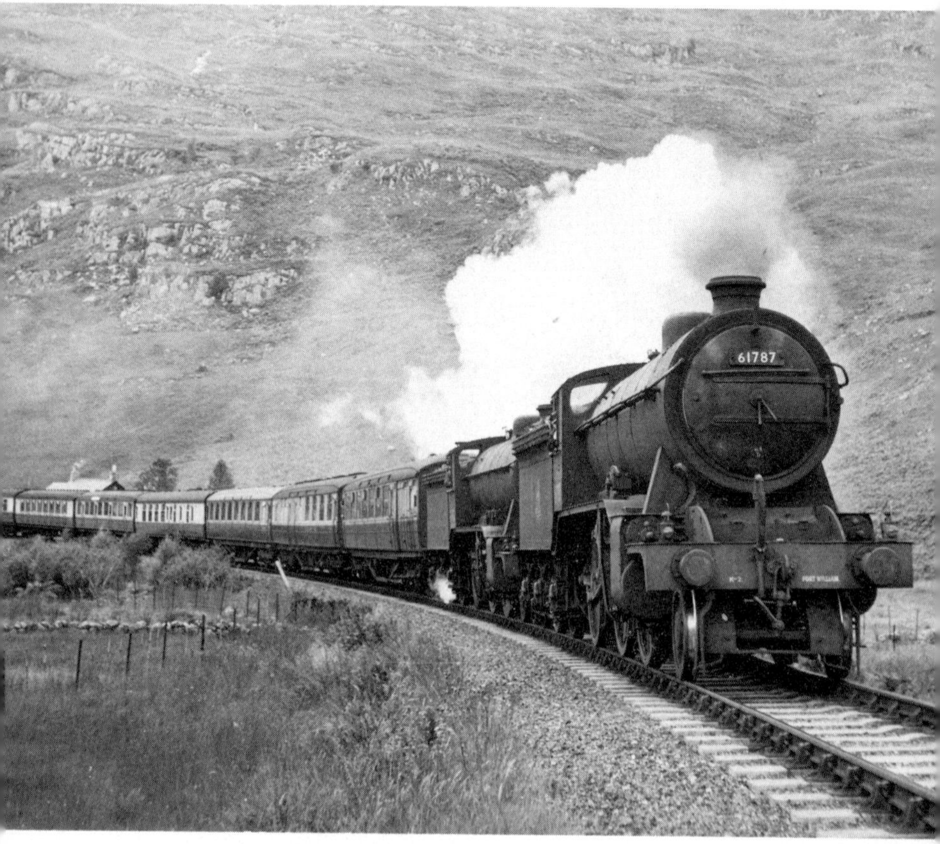
61787

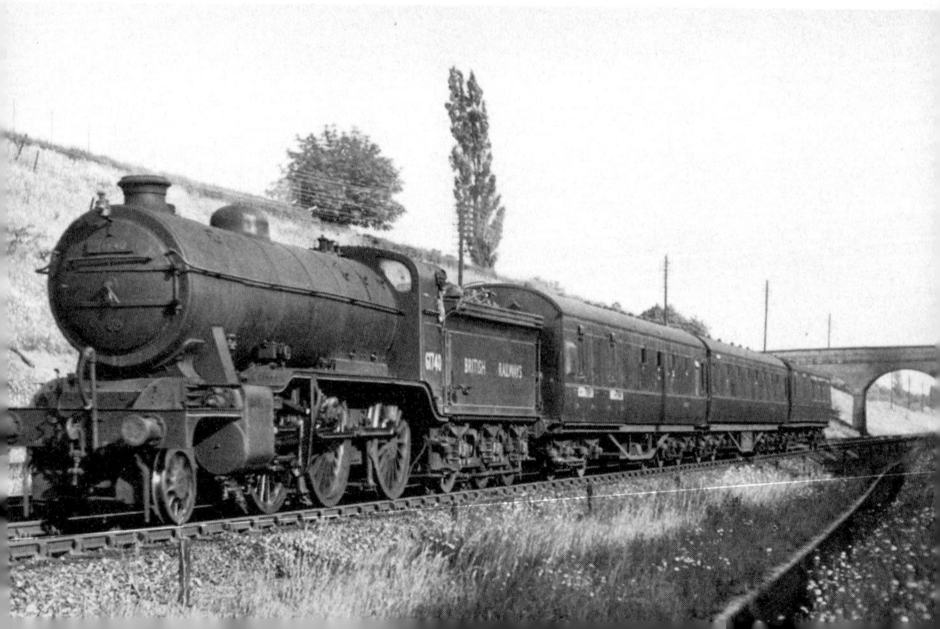
61740
BRITISH RAILWAYS

Left: Mallaig to Fort William train at Lochailort with K2s No 61787 *Loch Quoich* and 61788 *Loch Rannoch.*   Eric Treacy

Below left: K2 No 61740, lettered British Railways, near Edwalton with a Spalding-Nottingham train, showing M&GNR type tablet catcher. *T. G. Hepburn*

Above: The first GNR Class H4, LNER K3 class 2-6-0 No 1000 as first built in 1920, showing the outside marine type big end.   *Locomotive Publishing Co*

Below: GNR No 1000 at the head of a 75 wagon down goods train in 1920. Indicating equipment is in place on cylinders but the engine is not actually being tested.   *Locomotive Publishing Co*

Top: No 1002 on down express passenger train near Hadley Wood during the 1921 coal strike.   *Ian Allan Library*

Above: LNER K3 No 4007 standing at Grantham Yard Box c1930 with original cab and chimney.   *T. G. Hepburn*

Top right: K3 No 4000 in early LNER days with Group Standard tender at Doncaster c1928.   *T. G. Hepburn*

Centre right: K3 No 159 as first built by Darlington after grouping in 1925 with NER type cab and hydrostatic lubrication.   Photographed at Doncaster. *T. G. Hepburn*

Bottom right: K3 No 2935: one of the later Armstrong Whitworth-built engines of 1934, with the later type lagging over the smokebox saddle.   *T. G. Hepburn*

Above: K3 No 227 fitted with an electrical foam indicator in 1936, seen here at Doncaster. *T. G. Hepburn*

Below: No 1935 was painted in postwar apple green in 1947, the only green K3 in LNER days. *J. Cliffe Collection*

Above right: The Down 'Scotch Goods' near Potters Bar hauled by K3 No 113. *The late H. C. Doyle*

Right: K3 No 61869 leaving Outward Marshalling Yard, Hessle, with a freight for Gascoigne Wood. *R. K. Evans*

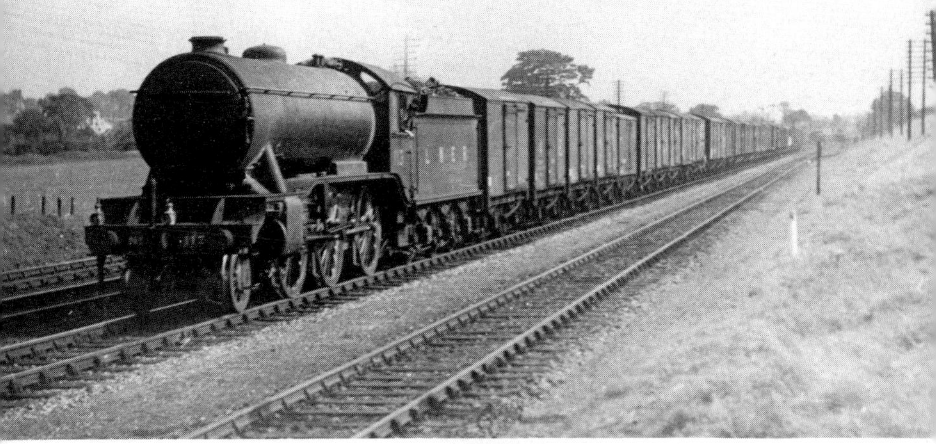

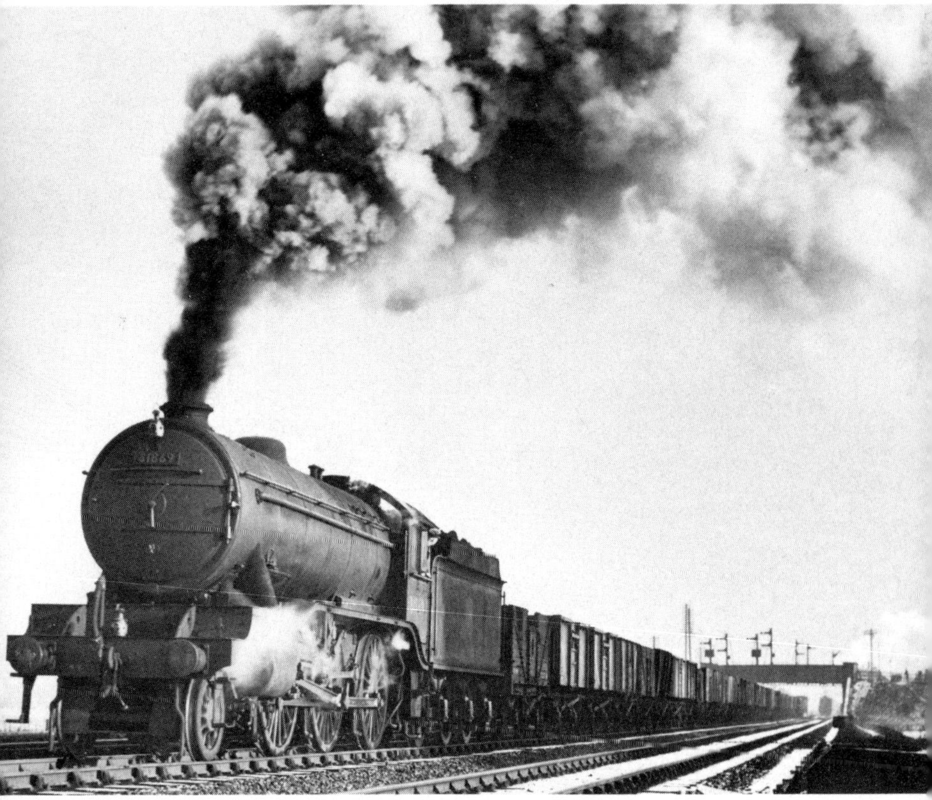

Top: K2 No 61740 and K3 No 61837 double head the Fish train from Grimsby to Banbury and the GWR into Nottingham Victoria in 1951.   *T. G. Hepburn*

Above: K3s Nos 61975 and 61883 double head the 'Banbury Fish' out of Grimsby in August 1956.   *J. F. Clay*

September 1946 (after No 206 had completed 50,000 miles)
Load 737 tons up, 422 tons down.

Engine	lb/ton mile	lb/mile
No 206	.103	58.08
50,000 miles	.120	67.65
	.110	61.78
No 2425		
42,000 miles	.120	68.24
	.111	62.95
No 2450		
50,000 miles	.120	67.01
	.115	65.99
Average		
No 206	.111	62.5
No 2425	.115	65.6
No 2450	.117	66.0

In accordance with the normal contemporary practice all engines had
live steam injectors only.   It was considered that No 206 had more
reserve power than the K3s, that it was better riding, and that it had
better accessibility, making normal maintenance easier.   On the other
hand it was added that the rebuild would be a longer time in the works
and repairs would cost more than a normal K3.   The increased boiler
pressure may have been a contributory cause.   No evidence strong
enough to justify further rebuilding emerged from these trials, the small
saving of less than 5 per cent in coal consumption would never recover
the costs of such a drastic rebuilding.   It was also recognised that the
rebuilding of No 206 had produced a nearly new engine.   No mention
was made of the additional stresses on the frames due to the stronger
thrusts of two cylinders, these doubtless emerged only after a longer
period in service.

There are two sides to all questions and the respective merits of two-
and three-cylinder locomotives was no exception.   No more K3s were
rebuilt as K5s and the remainder ended their days as three-cylinder
engines.   As steam declined so did the K3s and the Autumn of their
lives was in sad contrast to the dramatic early success of the clean,
green GNR 1000 class during the coal strike of 1921.   One of the last
K3 strongholds fell when BR 9F type 2-10-0s took over the Grimsby
fish trains in the early 1960s but right up to the last it was possible to
record the occasional surprisingly good run by a K3 especially on the
GCR.   The last K3 was withdrawn in December 1962 and none have
been preserved.

CHAPTER FIVE

Moguls on the West Highland

The West Highland section of the LNER was a railway where the difficulty of operation matched the magnificence of its scenery. It was built by a separate company, but from the first it was worked by the North British who absorbed it in 1908. The railway reached Fort William in 1894 and was extended to Mallaig in 1901. It was almost 100 miles from the junction at Craigendoran to Fort William and another 41 miles to Mallaig. A train from Glasgow traverses only a short section, that from Glasgow to Craigendoran Junction, on what might be called 'normal' gradients. The rest of line is characterised by steep gradients and severe curvature.

At first it was thought that trains would always be very light in such a sparsely populated area and that relatively small locomotives would suffice. The North British, however, designed special locomotives and coaches for the West Highland and in 1893 Holmes introduced the 'West Highland Bogies' ready for the opening of the line. These were 4-4-0s with 5ft 7in driving wheels. Any journey over the West Highland was, of necessity, a slow one, as stops had to be made and there was no scope for fast downhill travel to recover time spent in laborious climbing. The curvature limited downhill speeds to little faster than those attained uphill. It was barbaric to save weight by the use of light non-corridor stock so Cowlairs turned out a special series of coaches which were far better than most other NBR vehicles of the period.

By the Grouping of 1923 the West Highland standard passenger engines were the Glen class 4-4-0s designed for the section by W. P. Reid and built between 1913 and 1920. The majority were quite new in 1923. They were strong willing engines with an immense capacity for hard work, but they were only four-coupled engines and their restricted adhesion weight set a limit to their capacity on a route of such fearsome grading. Their maximum loading was confined to 180 tons which meant that there had to be considerable double heading. On such grades there could be no latitude and limits had to be strictly enforced. It was realised that, in time, standard LNER corridor coaches and sleeping cars would have to be used on some of the trains and these heavier vehicles would mean even more assistant engine mileage. Ideally a special type of locomotive, adapted to the West Highland, was the solution, but the immediate need had to be met by finding a class which could be permitted to run on the West Highland but which would allow a higher load limit than that of the Glens.

The replacement engines had to be six-coupled and they had to be a type which could be spared from their normal duties. The lot fell upon the former GNR K2 type Moguls. They provided a larger boiler and more adhesion weight which permitted the maximum passenger train loading to be raised from 180 to 220 tons. They could be spared from the GNR as new, larger, three-cylinder Moguls of Class K3 had been introduced in 1920 and were being added to by new construction from 1924 onwards.

In 1925 K2s Nos 4691-4704, all of the final batch, were transferred permanently to Scotland. They all had to be cut down in height before being accepted in Scotland. In 1931-2 another six K2s went to Scotland but these worked on the east side of the country mainly between Edinburgh and Thornton. They were accepted better than many transfers of 'foreign' locomotives in the early days of the grouping, but the spartan GNR cabs gave scant shelter in a West Highland winter and between 1932 and 1935 all the Scottish based K2s, whether working on the West Highland or from Edinburgh or Thornton, were fitted with side windowed cabs. In 1934 the 13 engines working on the West Highland all received names of Scottish lochs.

The load limit of 220 tons allowed some economies in working, as many trains with 'Glens' had demanded the pilot with only a few tons weight in excess, but the K2s did not find the West Highland easy. On the steep grades with their maximum loads they needed cut-offs of the order of 50 per cent or more and coal and maintenance costs were high. A more powerful engine was desirable as there was still quite a lot of double heading. The K2s had improved the operating position but they were not a final answer. The obvious choice was a K3 and the shorter GNR type tenders of some of the original GNR K3s were exchanged for the Group Standard tenders of seven Scottish based K3s. These made the engines shorter and would have allowed them to use the West Highland turntables but the K3s were rejected by the Civil Engineer on a weight basis.

Gresley pursued a policy different from that of the LMS who always tried to use standard types of engine on a difficult route or, if that was not a satisfactory solution, accepted double heading. The LNER was willing to build a small class of specialised locomotives for a difficult job. Gresley would use standard parts in a specialised design but not to the extent of adversely affecting performance. He had built the Class P2 2-8-2s to work the Edinburgh-Aberdeen road and, at first, an eight-coupled engine was considered for the West Highland. This would have had the three $18\frac{1}{2} \times 26$in cylinders of the O2 class 2-8-0 but with larger driving wheels of 5ft 2in diameter and a specially designed boiler aimed at keeping weight within limits. The boiler would have been tapered from 5ft 6in at the firebox end to 5ft 0in at the smokebox It was, however, rejected by the Civil Engineer on account of weight and length. In view of the problems faced by the 2-8-2 P2s on the Aberdeen road the rejection was perhaps wise.

A second, six-coupled, design was prepared with the aim of obtaining the greatest power output possible within the BSU 14 British Standard bridge span loading. This resulted in a factor of adhesion of only 3.54 but this was adjudged to be acceptable with three-cylinder propulsion. The boiler was basically a B17 type with the barrel shortened from 14ft to 11ft 6in. The tube diameter was reduced from 2in to 1¾in and this resulted in an A/S tube ratio of 1/365 which was lower than what was strictly desirable, but the lower tube resistance was likely to result in a very free steaming boiler. It was more important on the West Highland to have a boiler which would stand up to a heavy drain of steam on the banks and which would recover quickly after an exceptional effort, than to seek maximum boiler efficiency under test conditions. It is nevertheless significant that the later built V4 2-6-2s were the most economical engines ever used on the West Highland which may well have been due in large measure to their radically different A/S tube ratio of 1/450.

Standard K3-type cylinders and motion were fitted to the K4s and these were not of the monobloc type as has sometimes been reported. There were minor changes in the outside steam pipe connections on the later engines, Nos 3442-6. They had Flaman type speed recorders like the A4s to assist in keeping within limits on the curves and Bowden wire control for cylinder cocks and sanding gear was adopted. The first engine cost £5,455 in 1937 and the later 1938 examples £6,145 apiece. The 5ft 2in driving wheels and a boiler pressure of 180lb gave a tractive effort of 32,940lb which was raised to 36,598lb when boiler pressure was raised to 200lb/sq in. The smaller version of the Group Standard tender which had been developed for the J39 was used. The first engine emerged from Darlington Works on 28 January 1937 and was named *Loch Long* No 3441. It was painted black but shortly afterwards was given green livery. Five more were added in 1938. They allowed the maximum load to be raised to 300 tons against 220

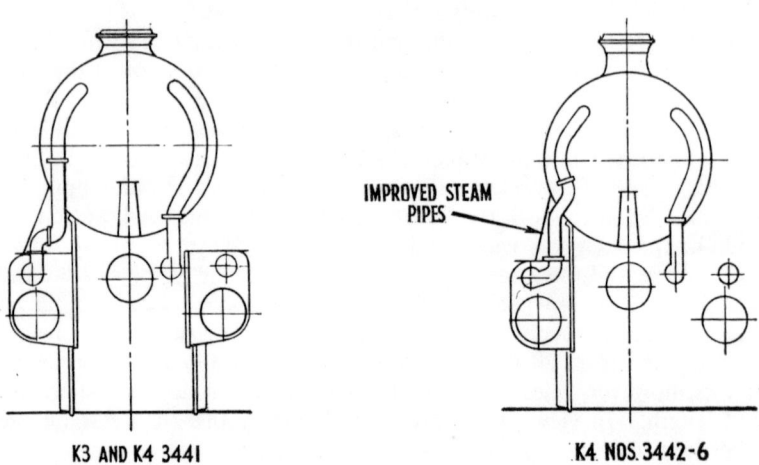

IMPROVED STEAM
PIPES

K3 AND K4 3441   K4 NOS. 3442-6

tons for the K2s. Their smaller driving wheels were a handicap on the fairly level section which was normally run at speeds of up to 60mph from Glasgow to Craigendoran Junction. They were so near to the permitted axle loading limits that double heading of a K4 was not permitted. It is true that loads of over 300 tons were rare in normal service but if such loads were needed at holiday periods two of the older engines had to be used. Similarly if a K4 was steaming badly it had to come off and by replaced by another K4 or by a pair of the older engines when an easier solution would have been to add the nearest available engine as pilot.

It may be asked how it was that so much more power was gained within much the same overall limits of size and weight without any unduly complicated design feature such as compounding. The answer lies in the specialised nature of the K4 design. The K2s and K3s were designed for mixed traffic duties over a wide range of loads and speeds. The K3s, as well as handling slow loose coupled mineral trains, were, in the mid 1930s, running daily at speeds of up to or over 70mph. The K4s were not true mixed traffic engines, they were built for the West Highland line alone and were intended to excel in slow slogging up very steep gradients.

The boiler of a K4 was smaller than that of a K3 and was only slightly larger than that of a K2, but the available steam was used to better advantage. To this end the tractive effort of the K4 was made very high in relation to the size of the boiler. Now tractive effort does influence the drawbar pull at starting and at low speeds even if it does not necessarily influence the maximum power at high speeds. A K4 had a tractive effort higher than that of an A4, yet the Pacific could develop double the horse power. The K4 had a tractive effort double that of a Class C1 Ivatt Atlantic yet it produced much the same maximum horse power. An express engine was designed with the aim of producing a high draw bar pull at high speeds and to this end it had to have a fairly large boiler in relation to its tractive effort. The GWR 'King' was a compromise in that it was designed to climb gradients, between Newton Abbot and Plymouth, as steep as those on the West Highland, yet it had to have a boiler large enough to allow it to perform well at high speeds. The K4 tractive effort approached that of a 'King' but its boiler was much smaller. As it had no high speed commitment, small driving wheels were acceptable, and this allowed the high tractive effort to be worked into a relatively small engine.

Although nominal tractive effort does not govern the power of an engine it does indicate the rate at which steam can be used and an engine with a high tractive effort can, within reasonable limits, use a given volume of steam with a better expansion ratio than one with a lower tractive effort. This governed the optimum speed range which was very low in the case of the K4. The practical result of this was that where a K2 had needed to be opened out to 50 per cent cut-off with full regulator on the steepest banks, a K4 would climb the same incline quite happily on 30 per cent. At a given rate of pound/steam per hour, the K4s would produce more dbhp at the speeds needed on the West Highland. Where the West Highland crossed the Caledonian Glasgow-Oban line at Crianlarich the LMS men would look with envy at the smaller K4 taking two more bogies away up the steep bank than their own 'Black Five' 4-6-0. The 'Black Five' was a general purpose engine while the K4 was a specialised design. The K4 certainly produced more draw bar pull at low speeds, but at 60mph or over the position was reversed. The Black Five's ability to run at 80-90mph on the Midland or LNWR main lines was irrelevant to the operating problem of the West Highland.

In prewar days on the West Highland the K4s were a great success. Reliable footplate observers such as O. S. Nock and the Canadian locomotive engineer E. H. Livesay rode on their footplates and retold their experiences in *The Railway Magazine* and *The Engineer*. It was a story of success that they had to tell. Mr Nock estimated that a K4 could do 50 per cent more work than a K2 on much the same coal and water consumption, and general confirmation of this comes from the official coal per mile figures. Scottish area K2s burnt an average of 68lb/mile during the years 1937-39 while the K4s, hauling heavier unpiloted loads, averaged 58½lb. It is true that those K2s working on the eastern side of Scotland are included in this figure but this would be more likely to lower the average than to raise it to a figure higher than that for the very hard West Highland alone. If the economies resulting from the elimination of much of the double heading are also considered, the K4 design was a true success.

When new, at normal hill climbing speeds, the riding of the K4s was reasonably good and this was mentioned by E. H. Livesay. When an engine was run down however, it deteriorated with high mileage and it could then be very unpleasant at 60mph on the more level stretch nearer Glasgow. P. N. Townend who rode on the engines in 1942 describes the motion as a vertical vibration, as if the whole engine was trying to shake itself to pieces, and this drove him to ride on the tender. It was in contrast to the rough sideways movement of the K2s which lurched from side to side forcing footplate passengers to hang on to the cab sides. The frames of high mileage K2s showed marks where the wheels had touched. Their's was the more typical motion of the hard slogging two-cylinder engine which contrasted with the high frequency vibration of the three-cylinder K4 working on a short cut-off.

The initial success of the K4s was, however, only short lived, because the outbreak of World War II in September 1939 brought an end to the world in which steam locomotives could be operated properly. Scarcely had the last K4 joined the others when war broke out, bringing lower standards of maintenance and poor quality coal. The sudden death of Sir Nigel Gresley in 1941 threw LNER locomotive policy into the melting pot. The Gresley locomotives had earned for themselves such a reputation in prewar days that every one expected his successor,

38

whoever he might be, would play the role of a Collett after Churchward and continue to develop LNER locomotives along the same general lines. The exigencies of war prevented Edward Thompson, the new chief, from playing the part of a Whale after Webb, but it was soon apparent that he had ideas of his own about what should be done in the future. Mr Thompson aimed at a high degree of standardisation, more like the Stanier policy on the LMS than that of Gresley, and he believed in simplifying locomotives as far as possible in the interests of more reliable running in wartime and in the conditions to be expected afterwards. He decided to use two cylinders instead of three in all engines except the very largest.

The K4s, being relatively small in numbers, were particularly vulnerable as there would be no place in the new scheme of things for a small class of locomotives which were now considered to be complicated for their size and expensive to maintain. Mr Thompson was also thinking of providing an alternative to the J39 class of 0-6-0 which was handicapped by its axle loading and would be unsuitable for further multiplication. He intended to build a standard 2-6-0 in its place when peace returned. One of the K4s, No 3445 *MacCailin Mór,* was due for heavy repairs and it was chosen as the guinea pig for experimental rebuilding.

No 3445 emerged from overhaul in December 1945 considerably simplified. The three cylinders with derived gear were replaced by two 20in × 26in giving much greater accessibility. The tractive effort was, of course, reduced, so, to compensate for the reduced cylinder volume, the boiler pressure was raised to 225lb from the original 200lb. A high boiler pressure in a locomotive intended for secondary duties is not an unmixed blessing but it was part of the price which had to be paid for the simplicity of two cylinders. The tractive effort was 32,081lb as against 36,598lb for a K4. To this extent the engine was less suitable for the West Highland. The single slide bar of the Thompson L1 2-6-4 tank was not used on the rebuild but the triple slide bars of Gresley design were retained. The boiler was a shortened version of the B1 boiler; in fact the K1 class had the same relationship to the B1 as the K4 had to the B17. The rebuilding was no help to the West Highland. It deprived the line of a useful engine because the rebuild was not intended for service on the West Highland alone, it was

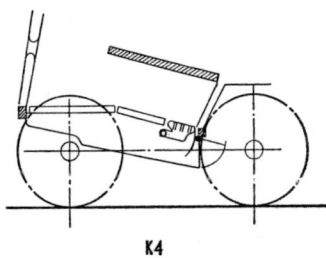

K4

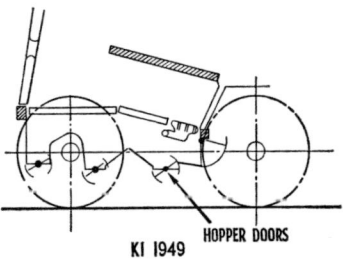

KI 1949   HOPPER DOORS

to be a general purpose type for use all over the LNER. It was transferred to England for trials and its performance was studied over a wide range of duties before it revisited Scotland. It was apparently satisfactory as in 1949 A. H. Peppercorn, who had replaced E. Thompson as CME, was allowed, under national ownership, to build 70 new 2-6-0s based on the rebuilt *MacCailin Mór*. These were built by the North British Locomotive Co and were given the larger type of Group Standard tenders. They were given BR numbers from the start, Nos 62001-62070; they were class K1 and the rebuilt engine No 61997 became class K1/1.

The standard K1s had a more austere appearance than the rebuilt K1/1 but they gave a solid and workmanlike impression. Their frames were deeper in front and the footplating was cut away in front of the cylinders making it easier to get out the valves for attention. The K1s had ample axleboxes of Pacific size, better than those of the B1s, and their rocking grates and hopper ashpans were a good feature in post war days. Their fireboxes had a staying weakness which was inclined to cause trouble in bad water areas. This was inherited from the B1 and the B17, and was connected with a reduced outside wrapper plate thickness. Flexible stays were provided, as with the L1 tanks, in the most likely breaking zones. An inspection plate was provided just in front of the safety valves and this can be seen in photographs. The single slide bar, as used on the L1 class 2-6-4 tanks, was adopted. Some trouble was experienced due to contamination of the exposed working surfaces. It was thought that some of the trouble came from brake block dust and a guard plate was fitted on some engines.

As with the B1s the Schmidt superheater and element fastenings was used instead of the Robinson type favoured by Gresley. The K1 boilers were built in two rings. In rebuilding the K4 to K1/1 Thompson had replaced double regulator handles with the conventional simple quadrant regulator handle. The swing link truck was replaced by the spring controlled type. Unlike the B1, the K1s were provided with adjustable wedges to the axleboxes, a legacy of their Doncaster origin.

When first rebuilt, No 3445 underwent trials against a J39 class 0-6-0 on the GNR and in Scotland. In January 1946 trials were run on coal trains and empties between New England and Ferme Park with Harworth Grade 1 coal. The results were:

	lb/mile	lb/ton mile	tons full	tons empty
K1 No 3445	59.9	.108	708	424
	59.0	.109	708	424
J39 No 2987	66.2	.118	717	428
	69.0	.120	752	428

The report said that the K1 was a good substitute for the J39, riding reasonably well during the tests, but the position when it had run

40,000-45,000 miles would need further investigation. An operational disadvantage was that it required a 52ft turntable and would not be able to use the 50ft turntable as could the J39.

In July and October 1946 the K1 was further tested in Scotland with similar results using Blairham Grade 1B coal. The engine had by then run 15,000 miles.

Thornton Junction-Dundee (300 tons)
K1 No 3445   58.5lb/mile
J39 No 4784   66.8lb/mile

Thornton Junction-Edinburgh direct
K1 No 3445   67.6lb/mile 516 tons
J39 No 4784   82lb/mile   554 tons

Thornton Junction-Edinburgh via Perth (170 tons)
K1 No 3445   46.1 lb/mile
J39 No 4784   52.6lb/mile

Edinburgh-Carlisle (433/464 tons)
K1 No 3445   .180lb/ton mile
J39 No 4784   .234lb/ton mile

On passenger trains in the Edinburgh area the K1 used 45.6 gallons of water/mile and the J39 55.1 gallons. On the West Highland the K1 could work freight trains up to the J38 loading. The J38 was a purely freight version of the J39 with smaller driving wheels. The comment was made that, throughout the tests, No 3445 handled its trains with greater ease and rode easily. The cab ventilation needed investigation and modification. The same turntable restrictions, as compared with the 0-6-0s applied in Scotland. The report was signed by E. D. Trask and was dated 5 November 1946.

No more K4s were rebuilt as K1s and they were restored to LNER green after the war, but their reign on West Highland duties was short. The criticism of the unsuitability of their small wheels for the Glasgow to Craigendoran stretch increased and they were withdrawn from the Glasgow-Fort William section but continued on the Mallaig extension. A batch of standard K1s was transferred to the West Highland and after the summer of 1954 the K4s ceased regular service, though they still appeared occasionally. They sank to miscellaneous freight and excusion work from Glasgow, which was a sad end to engines which had started with such promise. Had peace continued they might well have worked the West Highland with success for far longer.

Little has emerged as to the performance of the standard K1s but through the kindness of F. G. Cockman we are able to give details of a run which he timed from the footplate.

The K1 ran very well and the boiler rallied immediately after long bouts of full regulator and 45 per cent cut-off. The nature of the road was emphasised by the presence of check rails on many of the curves, this was a safety precaution when descending but added to the running resistance uphill. Comparisons with other straight inclines of equal severity may be misleading. The engine 'shouldered' when working hard and slowly, while the springing was hard, though no harder than some other engines on which Mr Cockman has ridden. The firing was little and often, after six well distributed shovelfuls were added the exhaust burned clear in 200 yards. The live steam injector gave some trouble but it was persuaded to behave better by taps to the clack with a spanner. This attention would have been less easy had the engine been fitted with top feed in the LMS manner. The load was, however, not comparable with some prewar K4 timings but the K1 proved to be a willing and competent engine. Full tabulation of journeys on the West Highland means little, as point-to-point timings are only comparable with those on the same route and a truly comparable K4 timing is not available. Brief details are however given below.

13.00 Mallaig-Fort William
Loco No 62031; 212 tons tare, 220 gross.
Driver McLean of Fort William, 8 May 1956.

Miles	Station	Sched (min)	Actual (min sec)	Speeds (mph)	Gradient	Boiler pressure (lb/sq in)
0.0	Mallaig			36	1 in 98 rising	225
				33	1 in 50 rising	
2.75	Morar	8	7 27			
				32	1 in 50 rising	
4.75	Arisaig	12	10 39			
				24	1 in 49 rising	
				28	1 in 90 rising	
				31	1 in 260 rising	
8.25	Lochailort	19	19 24			
				26	1 in 48 rising	
				23	1 in 48 rising	
				32	1 in 50 falling	225
9.0	Glenfinnan	20	21 32			
				35		
				24	1 in 48 rising	175
				42	1 in 60 falling	
				47	1 in 60 falling	225
6.75	Locheilside	13	13 03			
				35	1 in 260 falling	
5.0	Corpach		12 29			
				39	Level	
1.75	Banavie	4	3 40			
						225
3.5	Fort William	6	5 33			

Safety valves lifted at 225lb. Minimum steam pressure 175lb. Maximum cut-off 45%.

The V4 class 2-6-2s were used on the West Highland but they were limited to 250 tons against the K4 limit of 300 tons. These Rolls-Royces among mixed traffic engines were, however, the smoothest running engines ever to have run on the West Highland and the most economical. They were faster on the easier section nearer Glasgow than any of the Moguls. There had been some relaxation of restrictions during the war and 2-8-0s were allowed on the West Highland and after the war 4-6-0s were allowed. The B1s came first and in 1953 the Stanier 'Black Fives' arrived and later the BR 73s. These Class 5 4-6-0s were also limited to 250 tons, again emphasising the peculiar nature of the K4 design making it so suitable for the banks.

No general purpose engine used on the West Highland was ever able to improve on the K4 and double heading continued although larger 4-6-0 engines were employed. Long after the K4s had gone the veteran K2s, long past their best, continued to reinforce the 4-6-0s. Some LMR Ivatt 4MT 2-6-0s were tried but proved to be inadequate for the West Highland. The K1s displaced from the Glasgow-Fort William line continued to run on the Mallaig extension and finally diesels ousted steam all together.

The standard K1, derived from the rebuilt K4, became a popular engine for goods traffic elsewhere on the system. A good case can be made for the claim that they were the best LNER freight engines in their power class. They were a smaller version of the B1 4-6-0 and shared their qualities and defects. They had a similar reputation for rough riding when due for shops and this affected their performance on fast passenger trains when they were called on to assist at times of heavy traffic. They did very well in the hands of determined crews especially on the GER. At Stratford they acquired the nickname of 'Baby Bongos' which had even less dignity than the name 'Baby Scot' which so outraged the LMS establishment over a quarter of a century earlier.

CHAPTER SIX

Mogul Performance

The Great Northern Class H2 2-6-0s began quietly enough on the duties for which they were designed. They took over fast goods trains formerly worked by the 5ft 8in wheeled 0-6-0s. Among these was the nightly fast goods run to Doncaster involving a lodging turn for the men. No 1630 was allocated to Kings Cross and was seen on the 17.05 semi-fast outer suburban train. The Swindon dynamometer car was borrowed from the GWR and test runs were made on fast goods trains loaded to 57 vans and a brake. These were officially described as 'successful' but following the normal practice of those days, details were not published. They took their turns on excursion trains, such as the cheap trips to Skegness as had the 0-6-0s before them. They occasionally worked express passenger trains in emergencies but the aim of the design was not high speed and little emerged to suggest that their true vocation lay outside the description ' express goods engines'. They were used to good effect for ambulance trains in the early days of World War I.

By 1914 they had been joined by the larger boilered Class H3 2-6-0s and these followed the same general pattern of work. It was claimed that one had reached a speed of 75mph on a special test but drivers were reluctant to run either large or small boilered 2-6-0s at very high speeds. The GNR enginemen were a hardened lot with experience of Atlantics and of 0-6-0s at quite high speeds and they soon realised that an era of cushioned ease had not arrived with the new chief's initial designs. There was soon a lot of goods work for the new engines on wartime service and they rarely had to deputise for an Atlantic.

An 'express' run was recorded just after the war, in 1919, long before train services had returned to anything approaching normality. The late C. J. Allen described a run by 1645 in a summary of heavy loaded performances given in the August 1921 issue of *The Railway Magazine*. The load was 443 tons tare, 490 tons full, and No 1645 passed Potters Bar in 25½min and Peterborough in 103min 20sec for the 76.4 miles, having just touched 60mph on the descent from Stevenage. Stoke Box was passed at 29½mph in plenty of time for a punctual arrival on the very easy schedule of 148min to Grantham. Mr Allen thought that the very slow approach to both Grantham and Peterborough was due to the driver being more familiar with loose-coupled freight working. This slow approach made the arrival half a minute late but although this was a very slow journey for an express passenger train it would have been a good speed for a fast goods.

When the larger three-cylinder 2-6-0s of GN Class H4 were introduced in 1920 the two-cylinder Moguls were somewhat overshadowed. They did their share of work in the emergency of the 1921 coal strike and three, fitted for oil burning, operated from Kings Cross. The 9.50 Leeds and Edinburgh and the 13.40 Leeds and York were usually hauled by 'Ragtimers' during the dispute, but the heaviest work was reserved for the new Moguls of the 1000 class. In freight service the larger engines took over the fully fitted freights, leaving the two-cylinder engines to work the partially fitted trains which were not quite as fast. As more Pacifics were built in the early days of the LNER and more K3s were added to the original GNR engines, the need for the two-cylinder Moguls to work fast passenger trains grew less, but there were the occasional shortages which brought them back and in the August 1926 issue of *The Railway Magazine* the late Cecil J. Allen described how he had seen a 'Ragtimer' dash through Hitchin at a speed 'not less than 70mph and probably more' with a 63 axle, 450 ton night 'Scotsman'. This would doubtless have provided a more exciting log than the leisurely progress of No 1645 a few years earlier.

The bulk of the passenger work of K2s on the GNR was on secondary, short distance and cross country services. The most spectacular run ever recorded behind a GNR two-cylinder Mogul was timed by the late Dr W. A. Tuplin and published in his book *Great Northern Steam* (Ian Allan, 1971). The run involved both the fastest start-to-stop run and the highest maximum speed reliably timed with an engine of this class. No 1685, hauling a nine coach load of 280 tons loaded, ran the 19.8 miles from Doncaster to Wakefield in 20min 20sec with a maximum speed of 80mph as they dived under the Midland on the approach to Sandal. It would appear that there was some unofficial incentive for the crew to make such a run with a type of engine notorious for its rough riding.

The K2s were used but not loved on the GCR. Some of their first appearances south of Nottingham were with Wembley Exhibition specials in 1924/5. These were Colwick engines and GCR men from Leicester or Woodford would act as conductor drivers. The GCR men took exception to the uncomfortable riding of the GNR 2-6-0s and urged the Colwick men to work their engines hard on the rising grades to allow more easy running downhill. This did not always prove practicable with loads of 9-11 corridor bogies. Former Loco Inspector P. H. V. Banyard recalls an excellent trip he had with No 4646 from Leicester Central to Skegness via Nottingham Victoria, Kirkby in Ashfield, Mansfield and Lincoln with 15 bogies. A pilot had been allocated but owing to some trouble it did not reach the station in time and No 4646 set off alone. It was in excellent condition with only a short mileage to its credit after shopping; it had been coaled with Leicester's best express coal and steaming was exceptionally free. There were no reversals at any of the starts and the banks were climbed in good style. Fireman Banyard had, however, transferred much of the good coal from tender to firebox and coal of a much inferior grade from Boston had to be used on the return journey. They managed to get through but with a show of fireworks on Mansfield bank and from Gotham to Barnston.

Colwick shed had some of the early allocations of the GNR H2 LNER K1 engines and they used these on turns to Ferme Park and it was fitting that some of the last to remain as K1s with the small boiler were working from that shed. These included No 4638 which was often used in the mid 1920s on the 7.36 Breakfast Car express from Nottingham to Leicester. The 13 minute booking from Loughborough to Leicester caused the exhaust of No 4638 to be heard for miles around and red hot smokebox doors were by no means unknown. One of the Colwick drivers was a noise abatement fanatic, he would have no wireless set in his house and even objected to church bells ringing in daytime after he had been on a night shift. It was a different story when he was at work for the miners trying to sleep as he pounded his K2 up the Leen Valley line with the Sheffield goods!

The K2s were regularly used over the GCR on freight workings; no K2 was allocated to Leicester but some were on loan at times or were on unbalanced workings. The K2s were also used on the Leicester Skegness workings from the GNR station in Belgrave Road and some of Inspector Banyard's experiences in later years when he was supervising the Saturday workings were very different from the excellent No 4646 on which he fired in his younger days.

Some K2s were allocated to the GER to reinforce the 'Clauds' and 1500s pending the building of a new 4-6-0 class. They were usually in the hands of express goods drivers who did very well with them when used to their discomforts. In prewar days they were rarely short of steam on the GER. Few passenger runs have been recorded but it is rumoured that speeds as high as those attained on the Doncaster-Wakefield section were reached on the Southend line.

Some details of a satisfactory run on the Cambridge line were published by Cecil J. Allen in the November 1931 issue of *The Railway Magazine*. No 4674 had a substantial load of 64 axles weighing 445 tons gross. They passed Tottenham in 12min 20sec and stopped at Broxbourne in 26¼min without having exceeded 54mph, but this modest start was inside the allowance of 28min. The continuation to Bishop's Stortford was equally modest with nothing faster than 52mph but the remainder of the run was quite smart for the load and the nature of the road. It may be briefly tabulated (see table opposite).

This was a good example of a mixed traffic engine working a heavy semi-fast train in almost copy book style. The K2s were not designed to work flyers, they had been sent to the GER to help on secondary main line work. The total gain to the engine on this run was 5min on an admittedly easy booking.

At a later date in April 1940 Mr Allen described a summary of runs timed by R. L. Harrison on the 8.35 from Bishop's Stortford to Brox-

K2 2-6-0 No 4674; Load 445 tons gross.

Miles	Station	Min Sec	Speed (mph)
0.0	Bishop's Stortford	00 00	—
5.2	Elsenham	9.00	38
9.1	Newport	—	61½
11.3	Audley End	16 40	
0.0	Audley End	00 00	—
7.3	Whittlesford	7 45	70½
		sigs slight	
14.0	Cambridge	16.55	
		16min net	

bourne. The load was usually 10 of the lighter GER bogies weighing 270-280 tons tare and around 300 tons gross. The gradients were in favour of the engine. The summary included 17 runs by K2s, 11 with B12 class 4-6-0s, 7 with K3s and one with a J39 class 0-6-0. The K2s made the fastest individual run and reached the highest maximum speed, but the one J39 run was faster than the average for any of the other classes and was second only to one K2 run in start-to-stop time.

Class	Number of runs	Average start-to-stop (min sec)	Fastest run (min sec)
J39	1	14 29	14 29
K2	17	15 07	14 23
B12	11	15 16	14 39
K3	7	15 34	

The fastest run by a K2 reached a maximum speed of 69mph as did the J39 class 0-6-0. Another K2 with a slower start and finish reached 75mph and had a start-to-stop time of 14min 31sec. Although these runs represented smart working they required little in the way of hp because of the falling trend of the road. In general the K2s proved to be more useful on the GER than the larger and more powerful K3s because of their superior route availability. In later years they were used on the Midland and Great Northern Joint Railway including the 'Swedie' as far as Leicester on its through journey to Birmingham.

As more V2s were built, the K3s and, in their turn, the K2s sank lower in the social scale and more and more of their duties were on loose-coupled freight. As they declined in status they were more neglected and in the latter part of the war and in much of the postwar era many were in a pitiable condition. They still dealt with a number of slow passenger workings and there were exceptions to the general rule of deterioration. An example was the occasion when Driver J. Storr of Boston shed made a trouble free run to Cleethorpes with a K2 and 15 bogies. As is often the case in similar comparisons, the former GNR men give the K2s a better word than those from elsewhere. Perhaps the firm, straight GN main line minimised their rough riding.

A former New England fireman sums them up as 'Good second rate engines' and this is probably as fair a verdict as can be expected; it was, after all, what Gresley designed them to be.

The first K3 was built in March 1920 and in little over a year they had made a dramatic impact on the railway scene by their work in the emergency of the 1921 coal strike. No 1000 was, however, put through some quite severe tests when first built. One of the easily timed up Leeds expresses was run from Peterborough to Kings Cross with speed varying only between 56 and 59mph. The load was not specified, but in 1920 a speed of 56mph over Stevenage would only be expected from an Atlantic with a very light load. In the 1930s higher standards prevailed and such a speed would be expected from an Atlantic with a 290-ton 'Queen of Scots' Pullman. No 1000 was also tested with 80 loaded coal wagons between Doncaster and Peterborough over the joint line and on one occasion took 91 wagons weighing 1,600 tons. This train was stopped purposely on a 1 in 400 gradient and No 1000 started again without difficulty.

The new three-cylinder Moguls were a great asset to the company during the 1921 coal strike. A reduced train service was in force and certain trains were combined into huge formations of 18-20 bogies. Atlantics could handle such trains well enough once they got going, but starting was very slow. An Atlantic would have needed assistance from Kings Cross to Potters Bar with such a train as the 17.40 down and a 1000 class Mogul with 60 tons adhesion weight and 30,000lb tractive effort was clearly in a better position to attempt the southbound starts from Grantham and Retford than an Atlantic with 36 tons adhesion weight and 17,000lb tractive effort. The 2-6-0s were able to start much more quickly and their maximum speeds were quite fast enough for the emergency timetables.

An excellent account of the working of these heavy trains was given by the late C. S. Lake in the September 1921 issue of *The Railway Magazine*. Mr Lake rode on the footplate of No 1006 from Doncaster to Peterborough with an 18 coach load of 545 tons tare, 605 tons gross. Time was lost by drawing up at stations but little could be booked against the engine which was run for the most part on 30-32 per cent cut-off with the regulator fairly well open to give a steam chest pressure about 20lb lower than boiler pressure. Boiler pressure varied between the narrow limits of 165lb and 175lb at which the valves lifted while steam temperature ranged from 650 to 700°F which is rather higher than some more modern locomotives tested at Rugby or Swindon.

The most interesting part of the journey was from Grantham to Peterborough. No 1006 passed Stoke Box in 'a trifle over 10min' at 40mph and reached a maximum speed of 76mph on the descent. Mr Lake described the riding at this speed as 'remarkably steady considering the high velocity'. Peterborough was reached in a start-to-stop time of 33min from Grantham. A confirmatory run was published in *The Engineer* in which No 1006 passed Stoke Box in

10min 21sec but, with rather slower running down the bank, the start-to-stop time to Peterborough was 36min.

After Peterborough Mr Lake rode on No 1007 which covered the 76.4 miles to Kings Cross in 95min or 90min net. An even better run was mentioned by Mr Lake on the testimony of the designer himself. On this occasion No 1007 had a load of 20 bogies, probably 660-670 tons gross, and the time was 91min against a schedule of 93min. During the 1921 emergency the K3s established criteria of maximum achievement for the class; future performance was largely a question of producing the same hp under different conditions. The start by No 1006 from Grantham to Stoke Box was far superior to anything that could be expected from an Atlantic with a similar load. A contemporary timing of Atlantic No 295 with a 600-ton train shows that the four-coupled engines were inferior in starting to the Moguls to the extent of about three minutes to Stoke Box. Later in the journey the Atlantic No 290 matched the time of No 1007, pass-to-pass, from Huntingdon to Hitchin.

After the strike the Moguls reverted mainly to the fast goods duties for which they were intended. The Pacifics were introduced in 1922 with the aim of combining the haulage capacity of a 2-6-0 with the speed of an Atlantic. At holiday periods K3s were called in to assist with express passenger traffic. The fast goods workings needed good locomotive work and a 600-ton load of four-wheeled wagons had a running resistance higher than 600 tons of bogie passenger stock. The 15.40 'Scotch Goods' from Kings Cross Goods to Glasgow was the fastest purely freight service of its day. By 1932 it had been accelerated to an overall average of 39mph with a start-to-stop run at 44mph from Peterborough to York. On this service a K3 could climb the 1 in 200 banks at 40mph, reach speeds of 60-65mph downhill and 50-55mph on the level. The K3s ran these trains and the Grimsby-Kings Cross fish trains with success for many years. From 1936 onwards the V2 class 2-6-2s took over the heavier duties but K3s continued on the fish trains until the early 1960s when they gave place to the BR 9F 2-10-0s and soon after, BR decided that it was more profitable to abandon its share of the fish trade.

The K3 design was multiplied after grouping and they were very useful stand-by engines at times of heavy traffic. They were not fast enough to tackle a streamliner, nor powerful enough to work the 550-ton up 'Scotsman' of 1938 with its even time Grantham-Kings Cross booking, but a well handled K3 had a sporting chance of keeping time on the more ordinary GNR main line bookings such as two hours Kings Cross-Grantham or 95min Grantham-York. Some good work was performed on the Sunday excursion trains. We are most grateful for some timings by R. N. Clements of K3s on the GNR main line and these, together with some runs published by Cecil J. Allen and others, make a fair summary possible. Mr Clements timed most of his runs from the footplate and he makes the significant remark that his runs show that the K3s had the ability to run when the driver was willing to accept the riding of the engine. Some of his runs include deliberate easings downhill.

Kings Cross-Peterborough (76.4 miles)

Engine	Load (tons)	Actual time (min sec)	Net time (min)	Source
1003	424/460	97 25	94	C. J. Allen Sept 1921 *RM*
4008	357/380	84 39	84½	C. J. Allen Aug 1926 *RM*
116	465/495	95 35	94¼	R. N. Clements
153	467/500	91 05	86	R. G. C. Stephenson *Gresley Observer*
4008	413/430	113 20*	83	R. N. Clements
143	430/460	95 25	82½	R. N. Clements

* very severe checks and wrong line working.

The run by No 4008, timed by R. N. Clements, included the highest maximum speed of 80mph down Connington bank after there had been severe delays earlier in the journey. In the opposite direction fewer timings are available.

Peterborough-Finsbury Park (73.8 miles) Sunday Excursions

Engine	Load (tons)	Actual time (min sec)	Net time (min)	Source
153	467/500	79 05	75½	R. G. C. Stephenson *Gresley Observer*
2427	479/510	81	78	*Railway Observer*

The run by No 153 was an excellent one with 500 tons. It would be equivalent to a time of 79min to Kings Cross. This compares quite well with other locomotives smaller than Pacifics such as 80min net by the former GCR B3 class 4-6-0 *Lord Faringdon* with 460 tons and 78min by the visiting GWR No 4079 *Pendennis Castle* with 475 tons in 1925. No 153 covered the 57.3 miles from Fletton Junction to Hatfield in 57min 3sec and the 41.5 miles from MP 62 to Woolmer Green in 36min 26sec. This run was an example of the same high ihp of 1,300 sustained, rising to 1,500 maxima, demonstrated by No 1007 in 1921 but now applied to a lighter load at a higher speed.

K3 class engines were frequently used on the 17.00 from Kings Cross which called at Hitchin. Some fast running was sometimes recorded over the 44.5 easy miles from Hitchin to Peterborough.

Hitchin-Peterborough (44.5 miles, Schedule 49min)

Engine	Load (tons)	Actual time (min sec)	Net time (min)	Source
156	445/470	49 50	47¾	R. N. Clements
135	500/530	47 15	—	R. N. Clements

Engine	Load (tons)	Actual time (min sec)	Net time (min)	Source
2761	460/490	49 10	—	R. N. Clements
163	473/500	49 25	—	R. N. Clements
226	475/500	44 45	—	C. J. Allen, *RM:* July 1932

Hitchin is of course at a higher altitude than Peterborough and the road is easy but the near even time run by No 226 was quite smart. Huntingdon, 27 miles from Hitchin, was passed in 26½min and Stukeley Bank was topped at 50mph while the maximum below Abbot's Ripton was 74mph. A speed of 74mph and a similar 50mph minimum at Leys were features of No 135's run with 530 tons, but the start was slower.

From Grantham to Peterborough timings by Mr Clements may be compared with the 1921 epics of No 1006.

Grantham-Peterborough (29.1 miles)

Engine	Load (tons)	Actual time (min sec)	Net time (min)	Max speed (mph)	Source
1006	545/605	33 00	—	76	C. S. Lake, *RM*
1006	547/610	36 00	—	71	*The Engineer*
134	500/530	33 00	—	70	R. N. Clements
112	331/350	35 25	—	67	R. N. Clements
4004	410/440	36 40	—	68	R. N. Clements
126	370/395	38 45	32½	78	R. N. Clements

The run by No 134 passed Stoke Box in 10min 5sec from the Grantham start. This compares well with the best starts by other locomotives.

Grantham-Stoke Box (5.4 miles, 1 in 200 rising)

		Tons	Min sec
K3	No 134	530	10 05
K3	No 1006 (1921 coal strike)	605	10 10
A2	No 2400 NER *City of Newcastle* (1923 trials)	520	10 01
A1	No 4472 Gresley *Flying Scotsman* (180lb)	520	9 30
GWR	No 4079 *Pendennis Castle* (1925 Exchange)	475	9 35
GWR	No 6018 *King Henry VI* (1948 Exchange)	530	10 08
SR	No 35017 *Belgian Marine* (1948 Exchange)	535	9 37
A4	No 4467 *Wild Swan* (Single chimney)	525	9 21
A4	No 4901 *Capercaillie* (Double chimney)	550	9 24
W1	No 10000 (Rebuilt)	490	8 07
W1	No 10000 (Rebuilt)	650	9 44
A1	No 60157 Peppercorn *Great Eastern*	500	8 05

Against such a galaxy of talent it is not to be expected that the K3s achieved record times in the absolute sense, but they compared well with any engine in the table on a size for size basis. The K3 had the advantage of no weight transference, owing to carrying wheels under the cab, and there was strong incentive to avoid having to run unduly fast downhill which tended to make drivers run hard uphill. A Pacific driver would normally let his engine make its own pace at the start in the knowledge that he could always let her run later. It was, however, by no means typical of K3 running that a brisk start would be made, none of Mr Clement's timings except this one involved a fast start.

The K3s did a lot of very good work between Leeds and Doncaster. The prewar timetable allowance was 25min for the 19.9 miles from Doncaster to Wakefield and, with loads of around 400 tons, time could be kept without difficulty but fast running downhill was needed and speeds of up to 79mph were recorded by K3s. Occasionally a special effort would be called for uphill and one such event is mentioned by the late Dr W. A. Tuplin in the *SLS Journal* and in *Essays in Steam;* Ian Allan, 1970. The driver of No 146 tried to top Nostell Bank at 60mph and despite a load of 410 tons he succeeded as far as can be assumed from milepost timing. On another occasion No 111 topped Nostell at 53mph with 430 tons. The rebuilding of Calder Bridge in 1937 allowed Pacifics and V2s to work through to Leeds but the K3s were not completely ousted until 1943/4. During the war R. H. N. Hardy rode on Nos 202, 231, 203 and 91 with loads of 17-18 bogies as far as Wakefield. The schedule was by then 27min but it was often done in 25min. The start was made in full gear but the engine was pulled up quickly and the regulator opened to full. Most of the work was done on 25 per cent cut-off with 30 per cent on the banks. Downhill 15 per cent was normally used until the regulator was closed near Hare Park. The wartime limit was 60mph but 70s were not unknown. Mr Hardy found the K3s easy to fire, the best results came from a well built up but not heavy fire well burned through and gently sloping with firing all round the box. The Leeds men at this time found the K3s very suitable for this kind of work. They were relatively light on coal owing to the light blast and very good front end. Leeds engines occasionally went to Kings Cross on excursion trains and there was a lodging turn to Whitemoor.

The K3s were at their best on the GNR on such duties as 14-18 bogies between Doncaster and Leeds, and former GNR men still give them a better word than those from other sections of the LNER. The GCR men would prefer one of their own B7 class 4-6-0s on a 10-11 coach Wembley excursion to the average K3. They would accept the heavier coal consumption of the 4-6-0s for the sake of their better riding. It is, of course, still possible to find former GNR men who claim that the GCR 4-6-0s were not always smooth riding and former GCR men who dispute the lower coal consumption attributed to the K3s. Naturally enough similar comparisons were made by NER men who preferred their own B16 4-6-0s. The K3s took over most of the express goods turns on the main line but the B16s retained the services to Ardsley, Hull and Whitemoor. The London fish trains from Grimsby, which had been handled by B7s, were re-routed via Boston and Peterborough on the much more easily graded GNR and were run by K3s. The selection of the easier route allowed maximum loads to be raised from 45 to 60 wagons but the change did not endear the Gresley engines to GCR men. On one of the Cup Final days in the early 1920s a K3 disgraced itself by failing on the GCR/GWR joint line with consequent delays to both railways and the story is still told with some relish by retired GCR men over half a century later.

In the early 1930s the northbound Penzance-Aberdeen was often worked by a K3 from Doncaster which was returning after working the Banbury fish. This train was frequently observed passing Quorn with rods ablur and they were doubtless whirling faster still at Lough-borough. A former GCR engineman, who is certainly not guilty of bias towards Gresley engines, confirms that near even time runs were made by Doncaster men with K3s between Leicester and Nottingham Victoria.

Confirmation that memories are not at fault was given in the December 1960 issue of *Trains Illustrated,* when Cecil J. Allen described a run timed by Wg Cdr J. M. B. Edwards on an RAF special which left Banbury 24min late with its 6 coach load of 220 gross tons behind a grimy K3 No 61967. Hopes of a sensational time recovery were low but the train was at Nottingham Victoria only one minute late on an easy schedule. The 45.2 miles from Banbury to Leicester were run in 49min 20sec after maximum speeds of 77mph at Braunston and 78mph at Whetstone. The 23.4 miles from Leicester to Nottingham Victoria were run in 26min 8sec or in 24½min net with a speed of 80mph at Loughborough and 76mph at Ruddington. Although the prewar Penzance-Aberdeen frequently loaded to more than 220 tons, the K3s of 1930 were younger and more spritely than they usually were in 1960 and there is no reason to doubt claims of fast running in prewar days.

In April 1961 one of the writers had a pleasant surprise on one of the GCR line semi-fasts. No 61913 was at the head of a load of 8 bogies and three four-wheeled vans weighing 298 tons tare, 320 tons gross. A smart start to Harrow in 14min 59sec was promising but then followed a series of checks. On the climb to Amersham speed rose on the 1 in 105 to 45mph. K. R. Phillips, who was an experienced recorder of trains on the Midland main line, considers that the 'Jazzer' was performing work comparable with the best efforts of 'Jubilees' and Class 5s between Irchester and MP 59¾ on the 1 in 120 on trains which had started from Wellingborough. It is not of course suggested that a K3 would be a suitable engine for the LMR XL timetable. No 61913 was restrained and delayed on the descent to Aylesbury.

The start-to-stop booking of 23min for the 21.4 largely uphill miles from Aylesbury to Brackley was an exacting one and No 61913 did remarkably well to make the run in 23min 37sec with 320 tons. This section is tabulated at the end of the chapter. From the Brackley start up 1 in 176 speed rose to 55mph and the 3.2 miles to Helmdon took 5min 35sec and 70mph was just touched before shutting off for the stop. The 9.8 miles to Woodford took 11min 55sec. The start from Brackley was comparable with anything ever recorded on the prewar 2.32 down 'Newspaper' which established such high standards of running with GCR B3 and LNER B17 class 4-6-0s. There was less interest about the remainder of the run with a special stop because of cattle on the line near Staverton Road and restrained downhill running below Ashby Magna. The K3s had a variable reputation on the GCR after the war but the driver described 61913 at that time as a 'good one', riding well and very different from many engines then considered good enough for the GCR which was deliberately being run down.

Nothing very remarkable was ever recorded by K3s on the NER but they equalled the best B16 running on the level between Darlington and York. They were usually employed on goods or secondary passenger work in Scotland. It might have been thought that they would have been better than a NBR Atlantic on duties involving strong hill climbing and moderate downhill speeds but a run in the Charlewood note books of a K3 deputising for an express engine over the Waverley Route was the reverse of successful.

Very little has been published of running by K3s on the GER but the Lowestoft and some of the March engines were kept in good condition and had a high reputation. A run timed by P. J. Coster in 1952 was a strange mixture. No 61951 had a load of 310½ tons tare and 330 tons gross, and where the K3 might have been expected to excel they did very badly. A combination of signals, and symptons very much like shortage of steam, made the train 17½min late at Shenfield after a most laborious ascent of Brentwood Bank. The engine then seemed to get a second wind and ran quite smartly from Chelmsford to Colchester. The start-to-stop time of 26min 10sec, 24½min net, was quite smart for the 22 miles and it involved speeds of 65-67mph.

Passenger and fast goods trains run at near passenger speeds were not, however, the only task of the K2s and K3s; they probably ran a bigger mileage on loose-coupled freights and in this capacity earned more revenue. In 1920 the new No 1000 was given tests on 1,600-ton mineral trains and the official verdict was that its performance was satisfactory. There was, however, no disposition to discontinue the building of 2-8-0 locomotives and Gresley continued to build these up to World War II and he experimented with the very large P1 class 2-8-2s. In 1931 there was the desire to speed up some coal trains between Peterborough and London so as to cause the minimum of delay to express passenger trains. These 'express' coal trains were made up of 56 loaded coal wagons, and one loaded bogie brick wagon weighing 50 tons fitted with vacuum brake was run next to the K3 class engine. They were worked under Class A regulations leaving Peterborough at 6.15 and 8.25 and were booked to reach Ferme Park in four hours or at an average speed of 18½mph including the time lost in stopping for passenger trains to overtake. An average speed of 20½mph was in force between Doncaster and New England. The empties returned to Peterborough in just over or under three hours averaging 24½mph inclusive of stops. The K3s were allowed to take 60 empties and one set of New England men could make the day's running without lodging away.

This running must have demanded some good work from the K3s on trains which weighed up to 1,100 tons. Some indication of the type of performance needed on loose-coupled freights is given in an account in *The Engineer* of a footplate run by the late E. C. Poultney on No 1001 soon after its construction. The load was 80 wagons, 21 open, 58 covered and one brake van, weighing 870 tons. Starting from New England yard No 1001 averaged 30.7mph from passing Peterborough station to Hitchin. Cut-offs were usually 30 per cent with steam chest pressures of 155lb uphill and 110lb downhill. Steam temperatures rose to 650-670°F. These working conditions were similar to those observed at higher speeds by C. S. Lake on the 1921 strike trains and as mentioned earlier, established criteria for the class. The 1000 class Moguls were clearly engines able to give much useful service to their owners.

The reputation of the K3s among amateur enthusiasts was quite high up to World War II although some complaints about rough riding had been heard on platform ends. It was something of a shock, however, that we read of a fireman who, in the November/December 1944 issue of *The Railway Magazine,* described the K3s as 'monstrosities'. A number of locomotive classes, not all from the LNER, were criticised in subsequent correspondence and it was admitted, even by the most critical, that the K3s were deficient in cab comfort and riding quality rather than in ability to do the job.

It was during the final years of the war and the first years of peace that the Gresley conception of three-cylinder propulsion was most seriously challenged and his successor, Edward Thompson, stood up to be counted as an advocate of two cylinders for all but the largest express engines. The two-cylinder K5, rebuilt from a K3, has left little record of performance but on freight duties, on the former GER, it has been described by R. N. H. Hardy as being little different from a K3 in general capability. This particular rebuilding can hardly have commended itself to authority, however, as no more K3s were converted to K5s.

The K1 class, introduced after experiments with the converted K4, have left behind a relatively good reputation but little or no recorded performance. They were, of necessity and by intention, mainly used on freight trains. Their 5ft 2in driving wheels made them less suitable for fast work but the exigencies of the service made them have to work fast passenger trains occasionally. R. N. H. Hardy considers them to have been extremely good engines for their intended duties and if in good running order, ideal as second eleven engines, ready to step in at times of heavy traffic to help the larger wheeled engines with holiday excursion trains on the GER to Clacton, Lowestoft, Yarmouth or Kings Lynn.

Mr Hardy found the K1s to be free steaming engines, easy to fire and this opinion is supported by former Loco Inspector Banyard from his GCR experiences and by K. R. Phillips from his occasional footplate experiences from New England Shed. Mr Hardy considered the K1 boiler to be a good one for maintenance and one that gave few other problems. He considered them easy to oil and dispose of, quick at getting away and sure footed. A Doncaster crew told K. R. Phillips that they preferred a K1 to a B1 on an all stations train from Doncaster to Sheffield or Hull.

No K1s were allocated to Stratford Shed but at holiday week ends it was usually contrived that a few were there to be 'borrowed' and without their help, traffic, especially on the Clacton line, might have been brought to a standstill. In prewar days the J39 class 0-6-0s had similarly to help out at busy periods and they were timed at speeds of up to 74mph on the GER but in the 1950s they had been banned from such work. The K1s were rough at high speeds but so were the K3s, B17s, B2s and B1s and very little time was booked against the K1s on GER passenger specials. Men would prefer one to a K3, which was never popular at Stratford. Speeds of up to 75mph were no problem with a good K1. On one journey with No 62040 Mr Hardy recalls going down past Witham at well over 70mph when the floor boards of this willing but very rough engine shifted and broke up leaving them to finish the journey perilously poised on cross members above the dragbox. There was little risk of falling through, but the journey was draughty and dusty.

The rebuilding of K4 No 3445 was of no benefit to the West Highland but the intention was to provide a general purpose engine for the whole system and this aim was successfully attained. The K1 class proved to be a very useful reinforcement to the B1s especially for their slower duties.

Kings Cross-Peterborough

K3 No 143; Load 430 tons tare, 460 tons gross.

Miles	Station	Min Sec	Speeds (mph)
0.0	Kings Cross	00 00	—
2.6	Finsbury Park	7 10	
5.0	Wood Green	10 45	46
		pwr	
9.2	New Barnet	19 50	37½
12.7	Potters Bar	25 40	37
17.7	Hatfield	31 05	69
		pwr	
20.3	Welwyn Garden City	35 55	36
25.0	Knebworth	40 35	51
28.6	Stevenage	44 20	

Above: K1 No 62031 working a Whitemoor-Temple Mills freight near Great Chesterford in May 1951. *K. W. Whiteman*

Below: K1 No 62040 passing through Colchester with a relief train from Clacton to Liverpool Street on 2 August 1958. *K. L. Cook*

Above: The 4.50pm Fort William-Mallaig train near Camus-Na-Ha hauled by K1 No 62011 with Ben Nevis in the background.   *W. J. V. Anderson*

Above right: The preserved K4 No 3442 *The Great Marquess* at Nine Elms Shed on 11 March 1967 ready for working a special from Victoria on the following day.   *P. H. Groom*

Right: No 3442 *The Great Marquess* attacks the gradient past Chinley North Junction with the Middleton Railway Trust's 'Derbyshire Dawdler' railtour from Chinley to Derby.   *Brian Stephenson*

THE GREAT MARQUESS
3442
L N E R

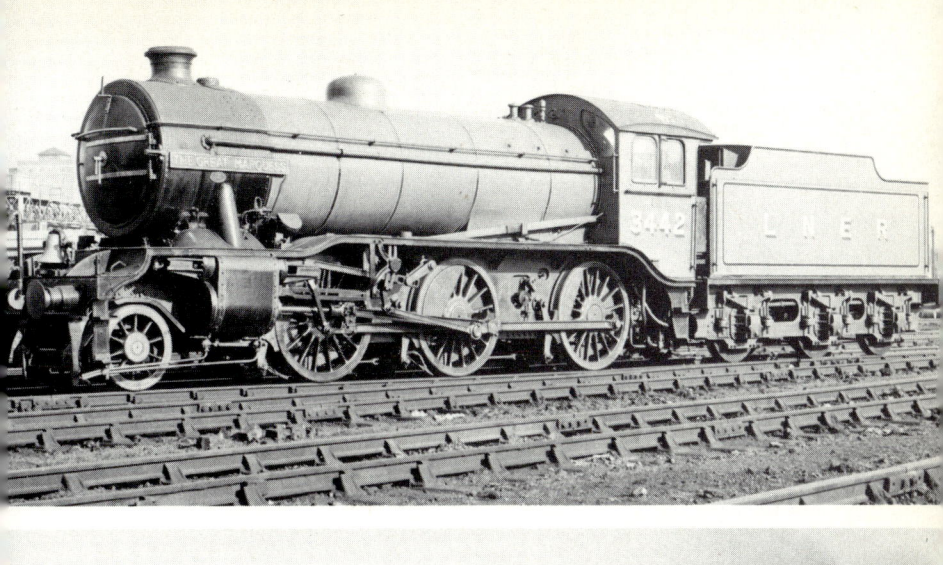

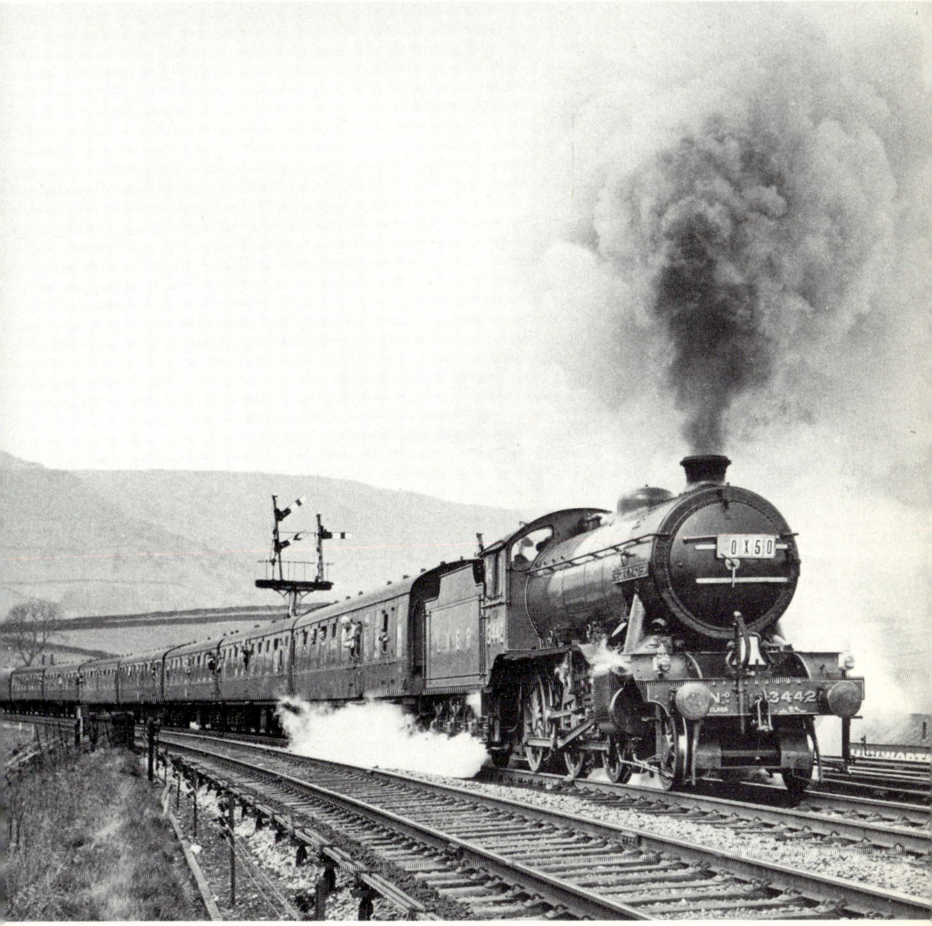
0X50
L N E R
No 3442

The preserved K1 No 2005 accelerates away from Whitby on 8 June 1975 with an excursion to Pickering. *L. A. Nixon*

Top: K3 No 61815 passing Colchester with the down 'Day Continental' on 8 September 1956. *T. M. Rounthwaite*

Above: K5 No 61863, two cylinder rebuild from Class K3 at Stratford April 1955. *Brian Morrison*

Top: The first K4 No 3441 *Loch Long* in original black livery at Eastfield in 1937. The steam pipe angle differs from that of later engines.
Ian Allan Library

Above: K4 No 3442, *The Great Marquess,* when new, takes water at Crianlarich on a Fort William-Glasgow train. *T. G. Hepburn.*

Top right: K4 No 61998 *MacLeod of MacLeod* lettered British Railways in postwar green at Crianlarich in 1950. *T. G. Hepburn*

Centre right: No 3445 *MacCailin Mor* rebuilt from K4 to two cylinder K1/1 at Eastfield in 1946, just before renumbering. *E. R. Wethersett*

Bottom right: Standard K1 No 62011 lettered British Railways at Grantham in 1950. *T. G. Hepburn*

Above: The rebuilt K1/1 crosses the Caledonian Canal on the 4.50pm Fort William-Mallaig in May 1956.   *W. J. V. Anderson*

Below: The 5.47pm train from Mallaig crosses the Loch-Nan-Uamh Viaduct in June 1954 hauled by K1 No 62052.   *W. J. V. Anderson*

Miles	Station	Min Sec	Speeds (mph)
31.9	Hitchin	47 20	72
35.7	Three Counties	50 15	78
37.0	Arlesey	51 20	73
41.1	Biggleswade	54 45	73
44.1	Sandy	57 10	70
47.5	Tempsford	60 00	70
51.7	St Neots	62 50	62
56.0	Offord	67 35	72
58.9	Huntingdon	70 10	63
62.0	Leys Box	73 20	51
63.5	Abbot's Ripton	75 45	
		sigs	25
69.4	Holme	83 30	64
		sigs	
76.4	Peterborough	95 25	

Net time 82½min; Schedule 90min.   Recorded by R. N. Clements

GCR Main Line   April 1961
K3 No 61913; 8 bogies, 3 four wheeled vans; Load 298 tons tare, 320 tons gross.

Miles	Station	Min Sec	Speeds (mph)
0.0	Aylesbury	00.00	—
6.2	Quainton Road	8 09	60/57
8.9	Grendon Junction	10 54	61
10.9	Calvert	12 49	64
16.6	Finmere	18 22	58/68
21.4	Brackley	23 37	

Schedule 23min.

Miles	Station	Min Sec	Speeds (mph)
0.0	Brackley	00 00	
3.2	Helmdon	5 35	55
6.8	Culworth	9 01	68/70
9.8	Woodford	11 55	

Recorded by J. F. Clay.

Comparative Timings
Aylesbury-Brackley
GCR 4-4-0 No 430 *Purdon Viccars;* 249/260 tons, 24min 25sec start-to-stop.
SR 4-6-2 No 34006 *Bude;* 360/380 tons, 21min 42sec start-to-pass.

Brackley-Helmdon
LNER 4-6-0 No 2841 *Gayton Hall;* 271/300 tons, 5min 35sec start-to-pass.
Speed at summit 55mph.

CHAPTER SEVEN

Moguls in Perspective

The Mogul type engine appeared first in Britain on the Great Eastern, destined later to become part of the LNER, as a goods engine with wheels 4ft 10in in diameter, resembling in size and power the large number of American 2-6-0s built for secondary and branch line services. This modest conception of the role of the 2-6-0 was carried further when Moguls, built in the United States, were imported for service on the GNR, GCR and Midland railways at a time of locomotive shortage. These had all very short lives but as they were being scrapped a new generation of 2-6-0 locomotives were being born on the GWR and GNR. The new Moguls were a uniquely British interpretation of the 2-6-0 theme in that they were intended for higher speeds than those run with any regularity by Moguls anywhere else in the world. European 2-6-0s followed the general pattern of American practice in that they were used on express passenger trains only if these were relatively slow.

The British Moguls, introduced on the GWR by Churchward in 1911 and by Gresley on the GNR in 1912, were intended for faster running, when required, than anything previously expected of a 2-6-0. To this end they were given driving wheels 5ft 8in in diameter instead of just under or over 5ft. During the grouping era many Moguls, all capable of relatively high speeds, were built by each of the four companies. The 2-6-0 type had its advantages especially in the impoverished days of the late 1920s and early 1930s. A 2-6-0 appeared to offer the promise of 4-6-0 performance, within its rather more restricted optimum speed range, for little or no more capital cost than a 4-4-0. A Mogul would take up no more room in a shed or at a station platform than a Midland Compound or a GCR 'Director' class 4-4-0.

The 2-6-0 in Britain started as a slow goods engine, experienced a re-birth in 1911/12 as a mixed traffic engine, rose to its zenith of performance and esteem in the 1930s and then gradually sank back to its original role as a goods engine. The last 2-6-0s built by the LNER, the K1s of 1949, had 5ft 2in driving wheels and the standard BR Moguls, some of them built in former LNER workshops and some running on LNER lines, were of modest design with 5ft 3in driving wheels. Before the end of steam the 2-6-0 had returned to its original conception of a secondary or branch line engine much like the American Mogul of half a century earlier. There had, of course been considerable progress in valve and front end design during that half century and the K1s and the BR Moguls could attain 70mph. When the Great

Eastern built Britain's first Moguls in 1878 there were not many large wheeled express engines reaching equal speeds.

The bulk of the work of 2-6-0 engines was never high speed haulage but the ability to reach high speeds was very useful, not only when a fast passenger train was hauled, but when a heavy fast fitted freight train was run at speeds not much below express passenger standards. This applied especially to the LNER who ran Britain's fastest freight trains. The LNER was however not alone in using 2-6-0 locomotives for fairly fast running for a number of years. The Gresley K2 and K3 class engines have been timed at speeds of up to 80mph and there is a rumour that one K3, running light during a bridge test, reached 90mph. There is a similar story of 87mph being attained under comparable conditions by a GWR 4300 class Mogul also on a bridge test. In neither case was the rotational speed impossible in the light of speeds of 85-90mph reliably recorded by BR Class 9F 2-10-0s with 5ft 0in driving wheels. The longer wheelbased 2-10-0s were probably riding better than the shorter 2-6-0s at such speeds.

Speeds of around 80mph have also been recorded by Moguls on other British railways including 83mph timed by D. S. M. Barrie, one of our most experienced recorders, between Winchester and Shawford by SR Class U 2-6-0 No 1805 assisting Drummond 4-6-0 No 446 on a nine-coach train. The SR Class U 2-6-0 had started life as one of the ill fated 'River' class tank engines and had wheels 6ft 0in in diameter. Perhaps more remarkable from the point of view of rotational speed was the same recorder's maximum of 82mph by an LMS Horwich 'Crab' 2-6-0 before Midcalder Junction. The 'Crab' had driving wheels 5ft 6in in diameter but it was assisted by gravity on a down grade of 1 in 100. The LNER Moguls were therefore by no means unique in their speed propensities, a modern front end livened up any engine's movements irrespective of ownership.

The SR built a number of Moguls with 6ft 0in diameter driving wheels both of two- and three-cylinder design and they used these for a time as the mainstay of the Waterloo-Portsmouth express services while others shared the Victoria-Eastbourne services. They were replaced by 'Schools' class 4-4-0s on both lines and the performance of the 4-4-0s proved to be much superior. The LMS built some 2-6-0s with 6ft 0in driving wheels in 1933/4 for use on the NCC lines in Northern Ireland. These proved to be very free running engines. The LNER never used driving wheels larger than 5ft 8in for 2-6-0s but they seriously considered a 2-6-4-4 type articulated engine with 6ft 2in driving wheels. The engine part of this was in effect a 2-6-0.

The LNER never used 2-6-0s regularly on an express service such as Waterloo-Portsmouth but on a shorter run over similar gradients, such as Doncaster-Leeds, they worked heavier loads. In occasional service, of course, K3s ran much longer distances such as Leeds-Kings Cross on excursion trains. The LNER Moguls were not unique in Britain for their high speeds but the LNER did have the most powerful examples of the type. No other railway combined a 6ft diameter boiler with 30,000lb tractive effort as was the case with the K3. There might have been a 2-6-0 nearly as large had the proposed Pickersgill 2-6-0 been built by the Caledonian in 1922. This would have had a 5ft 7in boiler and 28,624lb tractive effort. If the performance of other Pickersgill locomotives is taken as a guide the St Rollox engine might have pressed a K3 hard in slow slogging with a loose coupled freight but it would hardly have kept time between Grantham and York with a 500-ton East Coast express when deputising for a Pacific nor could it have skimmed along from Leicester to Nottingham in even time with the northbound Penzance-Aberdeen express.

The K3 had a claim to be considered as Britain's most powerful eight-wheeled engine and in the middle speed ranges this claim has much justification. In the higher speed ranges the honours would certainly go to the SR 'Schools' class 4-4-0s. A K3 could not be expected to reach 80mph on the level with over 300 tons but a 'School' would be most unlikely to pass Stoke Box in 10min 8sec from the Grantham start with 600 tons. The ihps needed for both performances would be similar but attained at different speeds. At 45mph on a rising grade of 1 in 100 a K3 probably was Britain's most powerful eight-wheeled engine but at 20mph on 1 in 50 it might well have been excelled by Gresley's K4 class 2-6-0 designed for the West Highland. At 80mph on the level the SR 'Schools' class with their 6ft 8in driving wheels and lower running resistance would take the lead. On a wet rail the greater adhesion weight of the K3 would be an advantage.

It may well be that no other British Mogul could ever have equalled the running of the K3s during the 1921 coal strike, nor could the nightly running of the 'Scotch Goods' have been matched. A more vital question is whether the K3s should have been built as 4-6-0s or as 2-6-2s. Was the 2-6-0 overgrown when extended to such size and weight? The reputation of LNER 4-6-0s in the same power class 6MT is shown by the nickname of 'Black Pigs' applied to the GCR B7 4-6-0s or 'Miners' Friends' applied to the NER B16s. The K2s were called 'Ragtimers' and the K3s 'Jazzers' and these appellations are equally significant. It is true that it is possible to find some loyal former GNR enginemen who will claim that these 4-6-0s were not always smooth riding and former GCR or NER men who say that the K3s were not so very much lighter on coal, but taking it by and large, the nicknames give a true picture. Those B16s which were rebuilt with modern front ends, either the Gresley B16/2s or the Thompson B16/3s, were of course very different engines which could be expected to equal the best thermo-dynamic performance of a K3 but no official figures are available.

It is an unfortunate fact that all LNER designed locomotives with driving wheels under the cab had a reputation for bad riding. The D49 class 4-4-0s and the 4-6-0s of Classes B17, B1 and B2 shared this criticism with the various Moguls. There is no certainty that, had the

K3 been built as a 4-6-0, riding trouble would have vanished. Gresley, however, accepted the fact that, as speeds were rising by 1935, something better than a K3 was needed as a running mate for the Pacifics. After considering a 2-6-4-4 with articulated tender and a 4-6-0 larger than the B17, he opted for the V2 class 2-6-2 for heavy main line work and for the smaller V4 for service anywhere on the LNER. The 2-6-0 was also eclipsed on other railways, on the GWR by the 'Hall' class 4-6-0s and on the LMS by the 'Black Fives'. The SR had not built the S15 class 4-6-0s in very large numbers. These were big heavy engines as restricted as the K3s and they only took over some of the duties from 2-6-0s but there was a general downgrading of SR 2-6-0s when the Bulleid light Pacifics were introduced in large numbers. BR built 4-6-0s of the 73 and 75 classes for the duties formerly carried out by 2-6-0s but they built Moguls for lighter work. The Class 9F 2-10-0s proved faster than had been expected and even after their brief but exciting spell on 80-90mph express trains was cut short by the authorities, they took over some fast goods workings including the Grimsby fish trains. Before the end came for steam LNER Moguls had sunk to work of a secondary nature. In 1921 when the first K3 was built there were hardly any express trains on the GNR which could not be run to time with no higher speeds than 70mph. In 1936, when the V2 was introduced, there were trains which reached 90mph every day and the three figure maximum was not unknown. No 2-6-0 could be expected to compete against larger and more powerful machines such as the V2s or the SR 'West Country' class Pacifics.

It may be asked if it would have been possible to have improved the riding of the LNER 2-6-0s by modifications to the design. In fact alterations were constantly tried without lasting success. The provision of axlebox wedges should have helped but when these were not correctly adjusted the situation was made worse. The fixed clearance box won elsewhere in the end but this did nothing to improve the B1s. All engines with a trailing coupled axle under the cab suffered to a greater or less extent. Even the GWR 'Kings', which ultimately became the best riding 4-6-0 in the country, required modifications and careful maintenance. There were only 30 'Kings' and they were always top link express engines which were given the best of attention. Where selected LNER 4-6-0s and 2-6-0s were given special treatment by crews and shed staff their riding was much improved.

In common with all Doncaster designed engines the LNER 2 6 0s had round top boilers. Opinion is divided as to the wisdom of this and the Belpaire boiler found favour elsewhere. In 1945 when the LNER were building LMS type Stanier 2-8-0s of Class O6 they estimated that each would cost £2,500 more than an equivalent O1 class 2-8-0 and they asked permission to build the O6s with the B1 type 100A boiler. Much later, in 1955, there was a converse proposal to rebuild B1s with LM Belpaire boilers. A different design team had adopted a different philosophy.

The K3 may be criticised with some justification on the grounds of its rather restricted route availability. As V2s took over the main line heavy duties it would have been useful to have moved the K3s to work on more lightly laid branch lines but their weight prevented this. The K3s were built to early too incorporate the latest thought on draughting and with hindsight it might have been possible to have built an equally powerful locomotive with a 5ft 6in or 5ft 9in diameter boiler and lower axle weight. This would have had a wider range of action but its lower adhesion weight might have been a disadvantage in wet weather.

The building of a small class of engines for a particular job was a typical Gresley solution to a local problem. The K4 class for the West Highland did their work well, but the case against the specialised locomotive was that it needed spares of its own, while a large standard class of engine could have plenty wherever it went. In practice it was not always as clear cut an issue; the K4 was built mainly of standard parts while a standard class such as the LMS 'Black Five' soon acquired a number of variations.

Gresley always stayed faithful to the three-cylinder engine for everything larger than 0-6-0s. This was criticised and his successor Edward Thompson adopted the opposite policy of only using three-cylinders when the engine was too big to do otherwise. Here again there are arguments on both sides, the greater accessibility of the two-cylinder engine had its attraction in wartime but the heavier thrusts of two large cylinders imposed a strain on the frames which was greater than that of a three-cylinder engine of equal power. The K5 rebuild from Class K3 was not multiplied. The heavier rods of a two-cylinder engine were more difficult to handle during repairs. Two-cylinder engines were not automatically cheaper on repairs than three-cylinder types. The LNER Peppercorn A1 class Pacifics and the SR Rebuilt 'West Country' class had slightly lower repair costs than the two cylinder BR 'Britannias'.

If the K5 rebuild was a failure, the K1/1 rebuild was a success, not that it provided a better engine for the West Highland than the K4 but in as much as it provided the prototype for a successful freight engine in the standard K1 multiplied by Peppercorn. The standard K1s gave much less trouble than the J39s they were intended to replace. The bearings and crossheads of the inside-cylindered J39 were all difficult to maintain. The K1 had ample axleboxes of Pacific size and better than a B1. They were ideal for slogging slow freight service. Rocking grates and hopper ashpans were good features in post war days.

It is always tempting to judge 2-6-0 engines solely on their high speed performance when, actually, fast running was only required during a very small proportion of their work. It is, of course, desirable that any mixed traffic engine could run fast when the call came and performance on passenger trains loomed large in their recorded history for the simple reason that it was more in the public eye than their goods train work, which may well have earned most of their revenue. The real test of the value lies in the contribution they made to the running of the railway. Compared with many other types the LNER 2-6-0s gave little trouble especially in prewar days. Their coal consumption was not above the general average and it was better than many locomotives of similar power. They ran good annual mileages for mixed traffic engines and they had low repair costs. Their boilers lasted well, as the majority had low boiler pressures and LNER water treatment was good. With hind sight we may claim that, notwithstanding their faults all the LNER Moguls gave good service to their owners. In modern parlance they were 'a good buy'.

Appendices

LEADING DIMENSIONS

Class GNR	LNER	Date	Driving wheel diameter ft in	Cylinders No	Dia (in)	Stroke (in)	Working pressure (lb/sq in)	Tractive effort (lb)
H2	K1	1913	5 8	2	20	26	170	22,070
H3	K2	1914	5 8	2	20	26	170*	22,070
H4	K3	1920	5 8	3	18½	26	180	30,031
—	K5	1945	5 8	2	20	26	225	29,250
—	K4	1937	5 2	3	18½	26	200†	36,598
—	K1/1	1945	5 2					
—	K1	1949	5 2	2	20	26	225	32,081

* Increased to 180lb with TE 23,400lb by LNER. † 3441 originally 180lb/sq in TE 32,940.

PROPOSED DESIGNS

		Date	Driving wheel diameter ft in	Cylinders No	Dia (in)	Stroke (in)	Working pressure (lb/sq in)	Tractive effort (lb)
2-6-0 Freight engine		1924	5 2	3	18	26	180	31,182
2-6-4-4 Articulated Engine		c1932	6 2	3	19	26	180	29,109
K6 Light 2-6-0		1947	5 2	2	17	26	200	20,330

BOILER DIMENSIONS AND RATIOS

Class	Grate Area (ft²)	Heating Surface (ft²) Tubes	S/H	Firebox	Tubes + Flues No	Flues Dia (in)	Superheater Tubes Dia	Type	Free Areas ft² Tubes	Flues	Total	Total % Grate Area	A/S Ratios Tubes	Flues
K1 (1913)	24.5	981	303†	137	125+18	1¾+5¼	1½	S	1.57	1.51	3.08	12.6	1:385	1:348
K2 (GNR	24.0	1,521	305	151	206+24	1¾+5¼	1½	R	2.59	2.01	4.60	19.2	1:385	1:348
LNER)	24.0	1,477	305	152	197+24	1¾+5¼	1½	R	2.48	2.01	4.49	18.7	1:385	1:348
K3	28.0	1,719	407	182	217+32	1¾+5¼	1½	R	2.73	2.67	5.4	19.3	1:385	1:348
K4	27.5	1,254	310	168	164+24	1¾+5¼	1½	R	2.06	2.01	4.07	14.8	1:372	1:337
K5	28.0	1,719	407	182	217+32	1¾+5¼	1½	S	2.73	2.67	5.4	19.3	1:385	1:348
K1/1 1945	27.9	1,240	300	168	141+24	2 +5¼	1½	S	2.44	2.01	4.45	16.0	1:320	1:356
K6 (Proposed) 1947	19.4	893	160	102.6	—	—	—	—	—	—	—	—	—	—

† Measured outside tubes.   S = Schmidt superheater, R = Robinson superheater

LNER 2-6-0 VALVES AND VALVE EVENTS

Class	Year	Valve Lap (in)	Lead (in)	Valve Travel (in)	Max Cut-off %	Exhaust Clearance (in)	Valve Dia (in)	Piston valve type
K1	1912	$1\frac{1}{4}$	$\frac{1}{8}$	$5\frac{9}{32}$	75	$\frac{5}{16}$	10	Schmidt trick port
K2	1914	$1\frac{1}{4}$	$\frac{1}{8}$	$5\frac{9}{32}$	75	$\frac{5}{16}$	10	Plain ring
K3/1	1920	$1\frac{1}{2}$ (c)	$\frac{1}{8}$	$6\frac{3}{8}$	75	$\frac{1}{8}$	8	2 narrow rings
K3/1	1921	$1\frac{1}{2}$	$\frac{1}{8}$ (a)	$5\frac{3}{8}$	65	$\frac{1}{8}$ (b)	8	2 narrow rings
K3/2	1924-25	$1\frac{1}{2}$ (c)	$\frac{1}{8}$	$5\frac{3}{8}$	65	Nil	8	Broad ring (d)
K3/3	1929	$1\frac{5}{8}$ outs	$\frac{1}{8}$	$5\frac{5}{8}$	65	Nil	8	4 narrow rings with ring control from 1932
K3/6	and later	$1\frac{11}{16}$ ins	$\frac{1}{8}$	$5\frac{5}{8}$	65	Nil	8	4 narrow rings with ring control from 1932
K4	1937	$1\frac{5}{8}$ outs $1\frac{11}{16}$ ins	$\frac{1}{8}$	$5\frac{5}{8}$	65	Nil	8	4 narrow rings
K5	1945	$1\frac{5}{8}$	$\frac{1}{8}$	$6\frac{5}{8}$	75	Nil	10	4 narrow rings
K1/1	1945	$1\frac{5}{8}$	$\frac{1}{8}$	$6\frac{5}{8}$	75	Nil	10	4 narrow rings
K1	1949							

(a) $\frac{3}{16}$in lead with $1\frac{7}{16}$in lap was tried on No 1009 in 1921.
(b) No 1002 was tried with $\frac{1}{4}$in exhaust clearance in 1922.
(c) K3/1 and K3/2 were subsequently given $1\frac{5}{8}$in lap, at first with 60% cut-off, later 65% restored.
(d) Broad and narrow rings were tried on successive batches.

Class	Year	Engine weight (tons cwt)		Tender weight (tons cwt)		Water (gal)	Coal (tons)	Brakes	Route avail- ability
K1	1912	61	14	43	2	3,500	6½	vacuum	—
K2	1914	64	8	43	2	3,500	6½	vacuum	RA5
K3/1	1920	72	12	43	2	3,500	6½	vacuum	RA8
K3/2	1924	72	12	52	0	4,200	7½	steam and vacuum	RA8
K3/3	1929	72	12	52	0	4,200	7½	Westing- house and vacuum	RA8
K3/4	1930	71	14	50	10	4,200	7½	steam and vacuum	RA8
K3/5	1931	72	12	51	9	4,200	7½	steam and vacuum	RA8
K3/6	1934	73	8	51	0	4,200	7½	vacuum	RA8
K4	1937	68	8	44	4	3,500	7½	vacuum	RA6
K5	1945	71	5	52	0	4,200	7½	steam and vacuum	RA8
K1/1	1945	66	17	44	4	3,500	6½	steam and vacuum	RA6
K1	1949	66	17	52	0	4,200	7½	steam and vacuum	RA6

ENGINE SUMMARY
GNR Class H2, LNER Class K1

Two outside cylinders, 4ft 8in diameter boiler. Designed by H. N. Gresley, first engine built Doncaster 1912, remainder built 1913, numbers 1630-1639. Rebuilt as GNR Class H3, LNER Class K2 between June 1920 and July 1937. Class extinct July 1937.

GNR Class H3, LNER Class K2

Outside cylinders, 5ft 6in diameter boiler. Designed by H. N. Gresley, first engine built 1914, last engine built 1921. Numbers 1640-1704. Class had 75 engines, including 10 rebuilt from Class K1.

Batches
1640-1659 Built Doncaster 1914-1917
1660-1679 Built North British Locomotive Company 1918-1919
1680-1704 Built Kitson and Co 1921
1630-1639 Built Doncaster, rebuilt from K1 to K2 between June 1920 and July 1937.

Withdrawals
First engine withdrawn September 1955, last withdrawn June 1962.

Renumbering
Nos 1630-1704 renumbered 4630-4704 LNER 1924.
Nos 4630-4704 renumbered 1720-1794 under 1946 renumbering scheme.

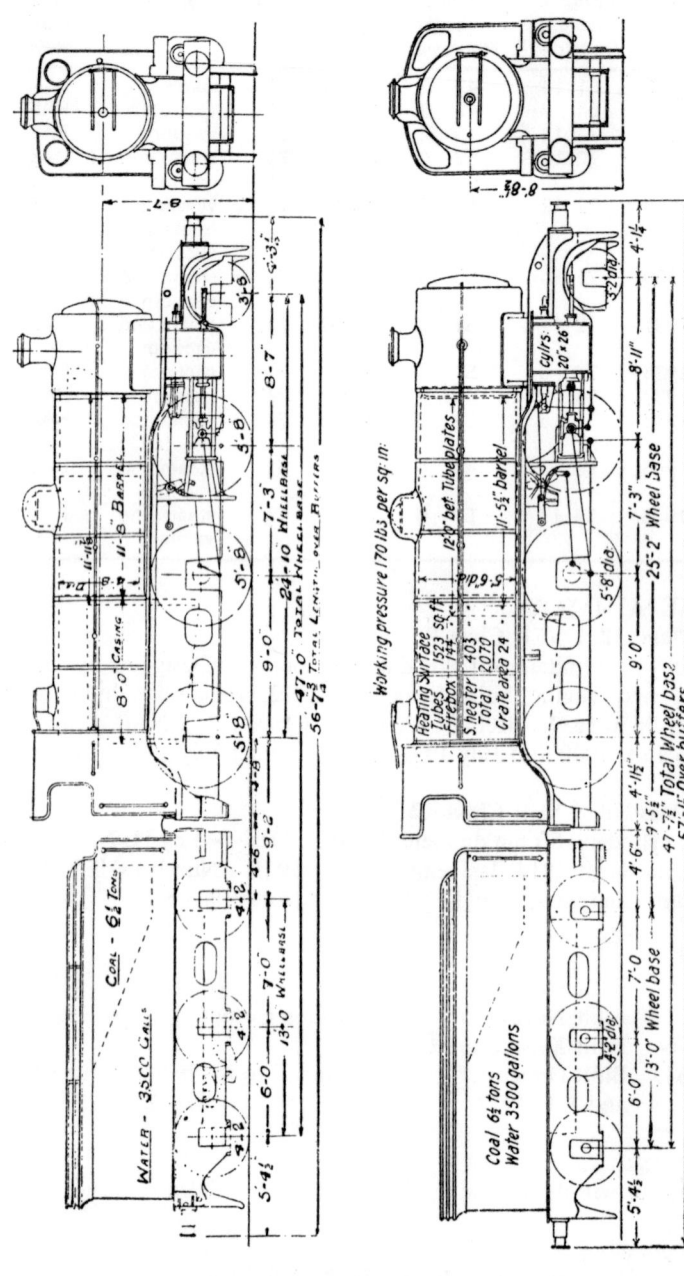

Top: Great Northern Railway Class H2 2-6-0 No 1630 in original condition (1912); LNER Class K1.

Above: Great Northern Railway Class H3 2-6-0 No 1640 an express goods engine (1914); LNER Class K2.

The prefix 'E' was added to former LNER engine numbers after nationalisation.
From March 1948 onwards 60,000 added to LNER numbers 1720-1794 became 61720-61794.

K2 Names

4674/1764 *Loch Arkaig*
4682/1772 *Loch Lochy*
4684/1774 *Loch Garry*
4685/1775 *Loch Treig*
4691/1781 *Loch Morar*
4692/1782 *Loch Eil*
4693/1783 *Loch Sheil*

4697/1787 *Loch Quoich*
4698/1788 *Loch Rannoch*
4699/1789 *Loch Laidon*
4700/1790 *Loch Lomond*
4701/1791 *Loch Laggan*
4704/1794 *Loch Oich*

Between 1924 and 1932 20 K2s were transferred to Scotland, 13 used in regular service on the West Highland line were named between February 1933 and June 1934. Curved nameplates were fitted over the middle pair of driving wheels. The 10 K2s used in the Edinburgh area remained unnamed. No K2 has been preserved.

GNR Class H4, LNER Class K3
Three cylinders, 6ft 0in diameter boiler. Designed by H. N. Gresley, first engine built Doncaster 1920, 10 engines built for the GNR and 183 by the LNER. Last engine built February 1937.

Batches

1920 Doncaster, Nos 1000-1009.
The LNER K3s were not numbered in a systematic manner.
1924 Darlington, Nos 17, 28, 32, 33, 36, 38, 39, 46, 52, 53, 58, 69, 73, 75, 80, 91, 92, 109, 111, 112, 113, 114, 116, 118, 120*, 121*, 125*.
* Built in 1924 but entered service January 1925.
1925 Darlington, Nos 126, 127, 134, 135, 140, 141, 143, 146, 153, 156, 158, 159, 163, 167, 170, 178, 180, 184, 186, 188, 191, 195, 200, 202, 203, 204, 206, 207, 208, 227, 228, 229, 231.
1929 Doncaster, Nos 1300, 1312, 1318, 1331, 1345, 1364, 1365, 1367, 1368, 1386, 1387, 1388, 1389, 1391, 1392, 1394, 1395, 1396, 1397, 1398.
1930 Darlington, Nos 2761-2766, 2767, 2768, 2769.
1931 Armstrong Whitworth's, Nos 1100, 1101, 1102, 1106, 1117, 1118, 1108, 1119, 1121, 1125, 1133, 1135, 1137, 1141, 1154, 1156, 1168, 1162, 1164, 1166.
1934 Armstrong Whitworth's, Nos 1302, 1304, 1308, 1310, 1324, 1306, 2934, 2935.
1934 Robert Stephenson & Co, Nos 1325, 1332, 1333, 1339, 1399.
1935 Armstrong Whitworth's, Nos 2936, 2937.
1935 Robert Stephenson & Co, Nos 2938, 2939, 2940, 1322, 1307.
1935 North British Locomotive Co, Nos 2425-2428, 2438, 2439, 2440, 2442, 2443, 2447, 2448, 2449, 2450, 2451, 2459, 2461, 2463, 2466, 2467, 2468.

Great Northern Railway
Class H4 mixed traffic
three-cylinder 2-6-0 No
1000 (1920); LNER Class
K3/1.

LNER standard K3 (1930)
Class K3/4.

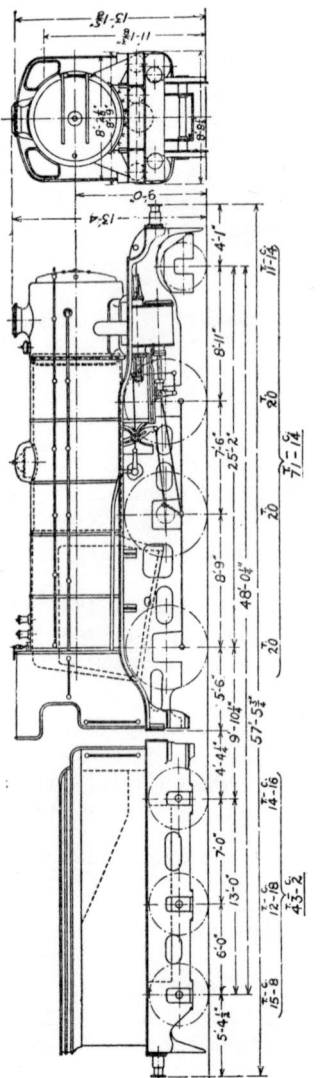

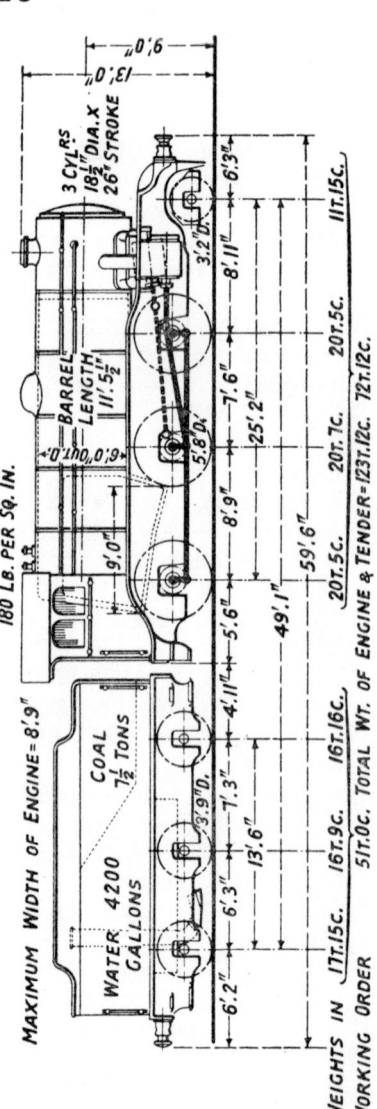

180 LB. PER SQ. IN.

MAXIMUM WIDTH OF ENGINE = 8'·9"

3 CYL.RS
18½" DIA.X
26" STROKE

BARREL LENGTH 11'·5½"

COAL 7½ TONS

WATER 4200 GALLONS

WEIGHTS IN 17T.15C.   16T.9C.   16T.16C.   20T.5C.   20T.7C.   20T.5C.   11T.15C.
WORKING ORDER   51T.0C. TOTAL WT. OF ENGINE & TENDER = 123T.12C.   72T.12C.

1936 Armstrong Whitworth's, Nos 2417, 2429, 2445, 2446, 2453, 2455, 2458, 2471, 2472, 2470, 2473, 2498, 2499, 3813, -3818, 3819-3824.
1937 Darlington, Nos 3825-3828, 3829-3832.

Withdrawals.
First engine withdrawn 1959, last engine withdrawn December 1962.

Renumbering
Nos 1000-1009 renumbered 4000-4009 in 1924.
Class renumbered 1800-1992 in 1946.
Prefix 'E' added to LNER locomotives after nationalisation.
60,000 added to LNER numbers from March 1948 onwards.

Rebuilding
No 206 rebuilt as two-cylinder K5 in 1945, renumbered 1863 in 1946.
Withdrawn as BR No 61863 in 1960.   No K3 has been preserved.

LNER Class K4
Three cylinders, 5ft 6in diameter boiler. Designed by Sir Nigel Gresley, first engine built Darlington January 1937; five more added 1938-1939.

Names and Numbers

No as built	1946 number	Name as built	Renamed
3441	1993	*Loch Long*	—
3442	1994	*MacCailein Mór*	*The Great Marquess* 7/38
3443	1995	*Cameron of Locheil*	—
3444	1996	*Lord of the Isles*	—
3445	1997	*MacCailin Mór*	—
3446	1998	*Lord of Duvegan*	*MacLeod of MacLeod* 3/39

No 3442 had its name, *MacCailein Mor,* incorrectly spelled and on arrival at Eastfield there were protests.   The engine emerged renamed *The Great Marquess* while correctly spelled nameplates were prepared and placed on engine No 3445.   The title *Lord of Dunvegan* was thought to be an authentic title for the chief of Clan MacLeod but it was incorrect and was replaced by the more truly Scottish *MacLeod of MacLeod* on No 3446.

Rebuilding
No 1997 was rebuilt with two cylinders in December 1945.   It was re-classified K1.   No 1997 was the prototype of the standard Class K1 and it was reclassified K1/1 in December 1946.   It was withdrawn in June 1961.   The last K4 was withdrawn in December 1961.
No 3442 *The Great Marquess* has been preserved and is at present on the Severn Valley Railway.

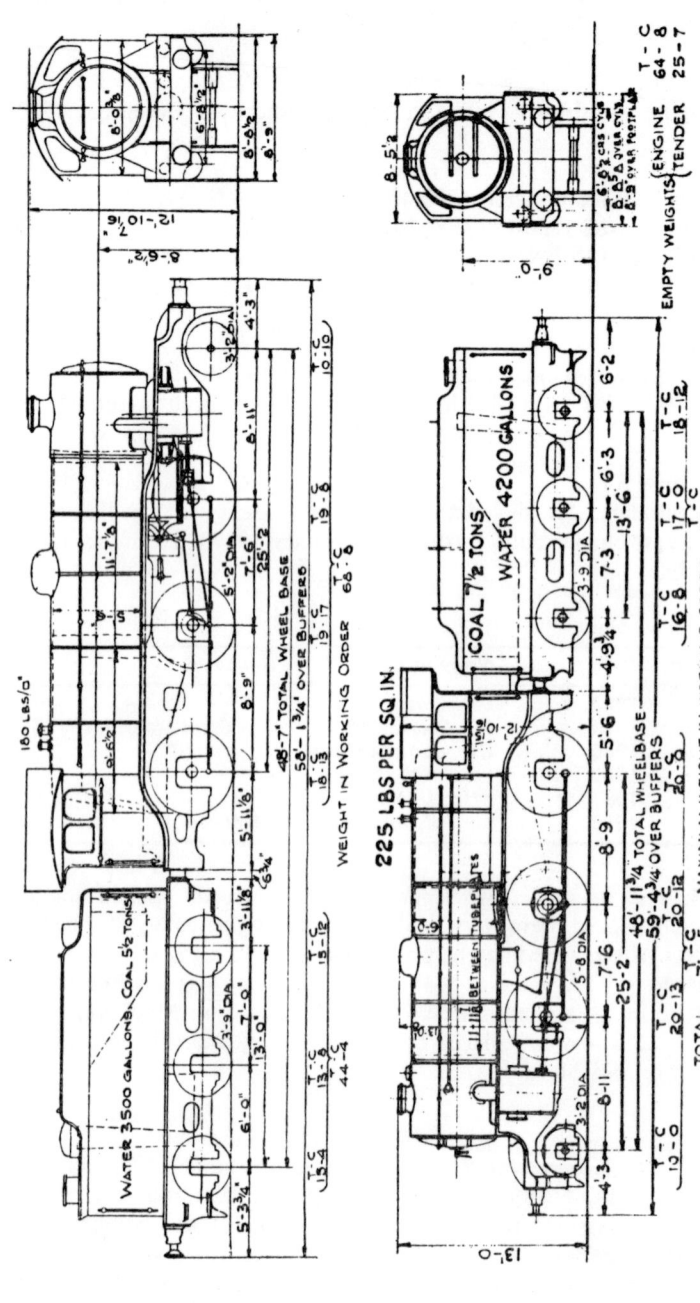

Top: LNER Class K4 three-cylinder 2-6-0 (1937).
Above: LNER K5 rebuild from K3 (1945).

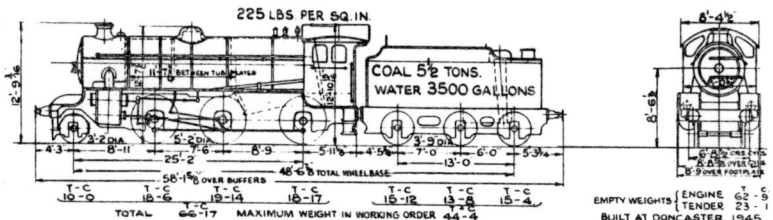

LNER K1/1 rebuild from K4 (1945).   Prototype for standard K1 (1949); built with 4,200gal tender.

LNER Class K1

Two cylinders, 5ft 6in diameter boiler,   Prototype rebuilt by E. Thompson from Gresley Class K4.   Standard class introduced by A. H. Peppercorn in May 1949 based on Thompson's rebuild.   Standard K1 Nos 62001-62070.

First engine built May 1949, last engine withdrawn December 1967. No 62005 preserved in LNER green numbered 2005 has been preserved and is at present on the North York Moors Railway.

TENDERS

The GNR K1s and K2s were fitted with the GNR Class B 3,500-gallon tenders.   They carried 6½ tons of coal officially but more could be accommodated by skilled packing.   The axle spacing was unequal with the first two axles 7ft apart and the rear pair 6ft.   The water pick up was operated by a lever.   It required, sometimes, the joint efforts of both men.   Some K2s used on the M&GNR section were fitted with tablet catchers located low down on the tender front.

The original 10 K3s Nos 1000-1009 were at first given GNR Class B tenders.   After grouping a new type of tender was designed at Darlington for the 50 K3s ordered soon after grouping.   This tender was known as the Group Standard tender but its NER origins were obvious. It held 7½ tons of coal and 4,200 gallons of water.   It had stepped out copings and unequal axle spacing with 7ft 3in followed by 6ft 3in. Weights varied slightly between batches but 52 tons was usually quoted. The first Group Standard tenders were not ready for the first two K3s which went into service temporarily with GNR Type B tenders.   No 32 was the first K3 to receive a Group Standard tender.   The GNR K3s Nos 4000-4007 were given Group Standard tenders in 1925 except for 4007 which retained its GNR Type B tender.   Seven of the GNR tenders were given to later K3s with the intention of using them on the West Highland line.   The shorter tender would have allowed them to fit the turntables but K3s were rejected by the Civil Engineer on a weight basis.   In 1929 the Group Standard design was altered to flush sides which appeared first behind No 1300.   Although this was a small modification the difference in appearance was considerable in that the tender now really did take on a standard LNER form different from obvious NER or GNR ancestry. The GNR type tenders stayed with their Scottish area K3s and GNR tenders were observed behind some Southern area K3s, Nos 80 and 91 kept them until 1942 when they and No 4007 received Group Standard tenders. Other K3s had tender changes of short duration.

A smaller version of the Group Standard tender was used on the K4s. This tender was developed for the J39 class 0-6-0 and carried 3,500 gallons of water and $5\frac{1}{2}$-6 tons of coal. The Group Standard tender of the larger pattern was used on the standard Peppercorn K1s. The self-weighing tenders normally behind B1s were used briefly for test purposes by K1s.

LIVERIES

The GNR H2 class, which later became LNER Class K1, were first turned out in GNR passenger colours of apple green with dark olive green edging. It appears that the first two H3s, which later became LNER Class K2s, were also initially in this livery. During World War I the GNR painted goods and mixed traffic engines grey as an economy measure and the 2-6-0s were included. New H3s were painted grey when built but the final batch, built by Kitsons in 1921 returned to GNR green. GNR engine numbers were on the cab sides in relatively small numerals and the letters GNR were on the tender. The GNR H4s, which became LNER Class K3, were also first turned out in passenger green. Their impressive appearance in this livery was shown in an excellent colour plate in the July 1920 issue of *The Railway Magazine*.

The LNER decided to paint all goods and mixed traffic engines black with thin red lining. Later the lining was discarded for freight engines but was retained for mixed traffic locomotives and was extended to secondary passenger classes. At first the lettering was L&NER on the tender sides with the number underneath. This was soon changed to LNER. The small suffix N was added to the numbers of all GNR engines but later 3,000 was added to all former GNR engine numbers. The 2-6-0s had all acquired lined black by the 1930s. From 1928 onwards numbers were placed on cab sides leaving LNER alone on the tenders. The batch of K3s built at Darlington followed NER practice in having 'Class 2-6-0' on the front buffer beams but later this was changed to 'Class K3' and in 1938 all LNER works were instructed to paint the LNER class number on all engines built or repaired. From 1943 the word 'Class' was dropped and the shed allocation painted on in its place.

When the K4 class was introduced in 1937 the first engine was black but the publicity people were conscious of the public appeal of the scenic West Highland route and the Scottish names of the engines. It was decided to paint all the K4s in passenger green.

LNER lettering was larger than GNR and there was attractive shading to letters gold on green engines and yellow on black locomotives such as the majority of Moguls. During World War II all LNER engines were painted unlined black with the letters NE on the tenders.

When peace returned the LNER made the bold decision to paint all engines green except the A4s which were to be blue. This proved to be an unduly optimistic gesture but representatives of many classes received the new colours. Before green paint penetrated far into the locomotive stock however nationalisation had taken place and LNER plans gave place to those of BR. A surprisingly large selection of K2s was painted green although this class had by then sank rather low in esteem. In proportion fewer K3 engines were painted green but No 1935 was included in a selection of green engines posed for an official photograph at Doncaster. The post war green livery differed from prewar in that letters were unshaded.

The BR livery for mixed traffic engines was black with LNWR style lining and the former LNER Moguls were so painted although one K2 remained green until 1954. The new standard K1 Moguls were turned out in BR mixed traffic black from the start. At first BRITISH RAILWAYS was written in full on the tenders but later the BR emblem was used. The prefix E was added to former LNER engine numbers but from March 1948 onwards 60,000 was added.

LOADING CLASSIFICATION

In the GNR loading classification the K1s and K2s were Load Class E1 and the K3s were Class E2. The letters were not in order and had no meaning outside GNR office routine.

The Southern area of the LNER adopted a system for freight train loading. This corresponded roughly with the LMS freight power classification but there was more flexibility in operation. The 2-6-0s were K2 Class 5, K3 and the two-cylinder K5 rebuild Class 6. The original Gresley K1s while awaiting conversion to Class K2 were power class 3. The standard Thompson/Peppercorn K1s were built in BR days and did not come within this classification. The K4s were built for a specialised job on the West Highland and were not classified for general use. They were allowed passenger loads of 300 tons against 220 tons for the K2s and 180 tons for the 4-4-0 'Glens'.

A statistical power classification based on the LMS system was introduced by BR. The K1 (standard), K3, K4 and K5 were placed in power class 6 and the K2 in class 4. There were obvious absurdities in this as for example when the K1 or K3 was placed in a higher class than a B1 at the passenger end of the MT scale. For goods services however the classifications were about right. The K3s were classed with the B7s and the B16s. The LNER Moguls were given mixed traffic ratings only, they were presumably only intended to work express passenger trains in emergency conditions whereas, in LNER days in the 1920s and 1930s, they had some regular jobs at quite high speeds. The 1949 classification was modified slightly in 1953 but the various 2-6-0s were left unchanged.

LNER 2-6-0 COAL CONSUMPTION AND ANNUAL MILEAGE 1936-1939

		Lb Coal/mile				Mileage			
Class	*Area*	*1936*	*1937*	*1938*	*1939*	*1936*	*1937*	*1938*	*1939*
K1	GN	55.3	—	—	—	36,954	—	—	—
K2	GN	62.0	62.0	61.1	64.4	27,471	28,692	29,330	28,494
	Scot	63.8	67.4	67.4	69.3	35,238	33,400	35,239	34,032
K3	GN	59.7	60.5	59.9	61.3	37,070	38,044	36,872	37,322
	GC	65.4	58.4	57.8	60.4	37,385	42,400	39,630	35,731
	NE	58.8	57.8	56.1	58.4	37,203	36,174	36,526	35,906
	Scot	64.8	64.7	64.8	63.4	39,602	42,242	37,018	39,347
K4	Scot	—	58.7	58.6	58.4	—	38,776	44,640	46,566

Engines of Comparable Power: GCR B7 and NER B16 were 6MT as K3s.

B7	GC	60.9	61.8	61.4	63.3	37,349	38,259	39,916	35,955
B16	NE	63.1	63.8	62.7	66.3	29,089	29,826	27,990	27,168

Comparable LMS 2-6-0, HORWICH 'CRAB', 10 Years Average.
Coal/Mile: 60.0lb.   Mileage: 34,635 Per Annum.
(*Chronicles of Steam;* E. S. Cox; Ian Allan, 1967)

Figures of coal per mile need to be approached with some caution. Locomotives engaged in freight service waste more coal while standing than passenger engines and annual coal/mile figures may depict the operating pattern rather than the locomotive efficiency.   When new the GNR 1000 class (later K3) on the 1921 600-ton coal-strike main-line passenger services were estimated by the late C. S. Lake to have burnt 51.1lb per train mile and .104lb per ton mile.   This was an excellent figure for such heavy work but the engines were, of course, nearly new and in good condition.   A run down K3 some 10-15 years later might quite easily burn much more in lb/mile on a relatively easy slow goods working with considerable waiting time.

ROUTE AVAILABILITY

At first the question of using locomotives on lines other than those for which they were designed was approached as the need arose.   There were cases of interchange of locomotives from the old companies such as the GCR 4-6-0s at Kings Cross and the GNR Atlantics at Sheffield but in the main LNER locomotives stayed mainly on their lines of origin.   In World War II there was the need for more extensive penetration of engines into new areas and a comprehensive system was evolved.   This was based on numbers 1 to 8 with the lowest numbers showing the widest route availability.   The system was revised for general use rather than a wartime emergency and the numbers were then 1 to 9 with RA9 applying to the largest locomotives such as Pacifics, Mikados and V2s.

The K2s were in class RA5, the standard K1s and the K4s in RA6 while the K3s were in class RA8.

The K2s had the same route availability as moderately sized 0-6-0s such as the former GNR J6s and the GCR J11s, the K1s and K4s shared the same restrictions as the J39 0-6-0s while the K3s were in the same RA class as the rebuilt NER 4-6-0s of the B16/2 and B16/3 classes. The original B16/1s in their NER condition as Raven built them were slightly less restricted in Class RA7 as were the former GCR B7s.

The K3s could use most of the GNR, NER and GCR main routes while there was a special dispensation in their favour on some GER lines normally RA7. There were additional restrictions which did not allow K3 and K4 class engines to be double headed on some lines in Scotland.

There was of course a good deal of useful work that the LNER Moguls could perform within their routing limits but by later standards they would be considered to be unduly restricted for mixed traffic engines. The B1 was RA5 and the two Gresley V4s were RA4.

UNFULFILLED PROJECTS
Gresley, Three-cylinder 2-6-0 Goods Engine, 1924
In 1924 a design was prepared at Doncaster for a goods engine to replace various pre-grouping 0-6-0s. One scheme was for a smaller driving wheeled version of the mixed traffic K3. The driving wheels would have been 5ft 2in and the leading pony truck wheels would have been smaller. The effect of this would have been to lower the centre line of the boiler allowing the larger chimney and dome of the GNR Nos 1000-1009 to be used within the LNER loading gauge. The K3 boiler would have been used but cylinders would have been ½in smaller. The combination of smaller driving wheels and smaller cylinders would have given a tractive effort only slightly higher than that of a K3. The cost of this design prevented its adoption and the cheaper J39 0-6-0 was built instead.

Gresley, Three-cylinder 2-6-4-4 Articulated Engine
In the early 1930s there was a need to reinforce the Pacifics at times of heavy traffic. This was done by double headed Atlantics or by over-loading single handed Atlantics or by making K3s run at express speeds. There were logical objections to all three methods and designs were prepared for building better running mates for the Pacifics. One scheme was for a modified K3 with 6ft 2in driving wheels but the larger wheels would have meant raising the centre of gravity of an engine already notorious for rough riding. Some experimental work had been done on an articulated engine and tender with some C7 class former NER Atlantics and this was to have been used in the new design making it a 2-6-4-4. The increased height would have meant an even shorter chimney and no dome at all. A domeless boiler would of course have been in the Stirling tradition. The disadvantage of such an engine would have been that it would have been less easy to separate engine and tender when repairs were needed and a minor defect in either would have put both out of use. The design was

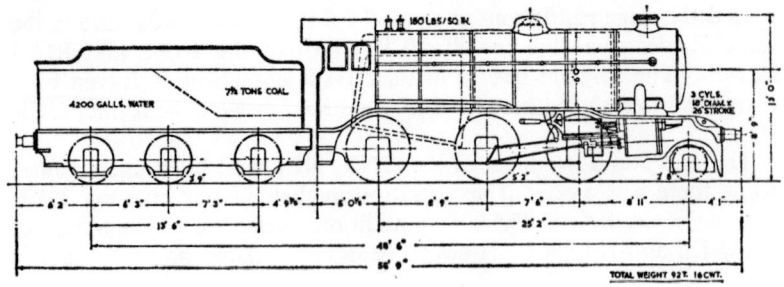

Three-cylinder 2-6-0 proposed in 1924 for slow goods services.

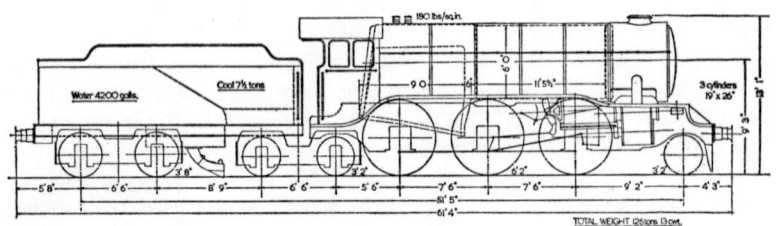

Three-cylinder articulated 2-6-4-4 developed from the Class K3 2-6-0 but not proceeded with.

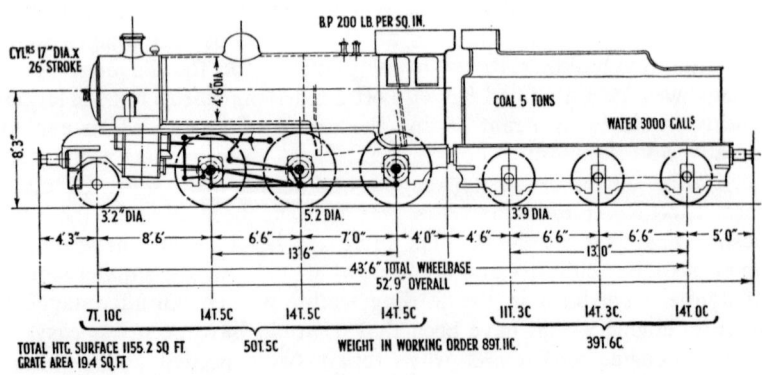

Proposed LNER Light 2-6-0 Class K6.

abandoned in favour of either a 2-6-2 or a larger 4-6-0 or both.   In the event the V2 2-6-2 was built in large numbers.

LNER Light 2-6-0 Class K6

Had nationalisation not taken place the LNER would have built a small 2-6-0 for service on lightly laid branch lines.   It would have had axle loadings of $14\frac{1}{4}$ tons and would have been midway in size between the standard BR Class 2 and 3 class 2-6-0s.   It would have resembled a smaller K1 with a tender cab.

LNER MOGULS, SHED ALLOCATIONS

The following tables show the allocation of Moguls at the end of the LNER ownership and under BR just prior to modernisation.

	Allocations as on 11/1/1947					Allocations as on 2/10/1954 (E&NER) 17/4/1954 (ScR)				
	K2	K3	K4	K1/1	K5	K1	K2	K3	K4	K5
Annesley	9							3		
Doncaster	11									
Colwick	23	6					19	8		
Immingham		11					7	13		
Lincoln		6					7	15		
Boston	6						12			
New England	2	39								
Woodford		15								
Sheffield								1		
Gorton								6		
March	8	25				25		42		
Norwich	6		1					9		
Lowestoft								6		
Colchester	5									
Parkeston	4									
Gateshead		9								
Heaton		12						9		
Hull Dairycoats		13			1			24		
Neville Hill		10								
Carlisle		10						8		
St Margarets		15						23		
Eastfield	14	2	3			3	10		4	
Fort William	7		2			2	5		2	
Aberdeen						1				
Thornton Junction						2				
Dunfermline										
Darlington						13				
Stockton						6				
Blaydon						13				
Haverton Hill						7				
Northallerton						1				
Tweedmouth								8		
Stratford								17		1

Bibliography

The Development of LNER Locomotive Design 1923-41; B. Spencer. Paper read to the Institution of Locomotive Engineers, August 1947. Reprinted by the RCTS 1947.

Locomotives of the LNER; K. Prentice and P. Proud; RCTS, 1941.

Locomotives of the LNER, A Preliminary Survey, Part 1. RCTS, 1963.

The Locomotives of the Great Northern Railway, 1847-1910; G. F. Bird; Locomotive Publishing Company, 1910.

Great Northern Locomotives 1847-1947; R. A. H. Weight; The Gresley Society, 1970.

From Stirling to Gresley 1882-1922; F. A. S. Brown; Oxford Publishing Co, 1974.

The Great Northern Railway: O. S. Nock; Ian Allan, 1958.

The Locomotives of Sir Nigel Gresley; O. S. Nock; Railway Publishing Co, 1945.

Nigel Gresley Locomotive Engineer; F. A. S. Brown; Ian Allan, 1961.

Great Northern Steam; W. A. Tuplin; Ian Allan, 1971.

Great Central Steam; W. A. Tuplin; George Allen and Unwin, 1967.

The Great Eastern Railway; Cecil J. Allen; Ian Allan, 1955.

The London and North Eastern Railway; Cecil J. Allen; Ian Allan, 1966.

Steam in the Blood; R. H. N. Hardy; Ian Allan, 1971.

Edward Thompson of the LNER; P. Grafton; Kestrel Books, 1971.

An Outline of Great Western Practice, 1837-1947; H. Holcroft; Ian Allan, 1957.

The Master Builders of Steam; H. A. V. Bulleid; Ian Allan, 1963.

The Steam Locomotive in America; W. J. Bruce; W. W. Norton and Co, 1952.

World Steam in the 20th Century; E. S. Cox; Ian Allan, 1969.

Maunsell Moguls; P. Rowledge; Oakwood Press, 1976.

Various issues of:
The Railway Magazine, The Locomotive, The Engineer, Railways, The Railway World, Trains Illustrated, Modern Railways, The Railway Observer, The Journal of the Stephenson Locomotive Society, Proceedings of the Institution of Locomotive Engineers, The Gresley Observer, Model Railways.